Whole food

THERMO

COOKED

Whole food THERMO COOKED

TRACEY PATTISON

MURDOCH BOOKS

SYDNEY · LONDON

contents

INTRODUCTION

I wholeheartedly believe that the foundation of great health begins in the kitchen. We need to get back to basics – applying traditional and simple cooking techniques, using real whole foods and choosing achievable recipes that satisfy and provide nourishment.

Getting organised and cooking food that will get your family eating at mealtimes, save time in the kitchen, not cost too much and improve your health and your family's health can seem impossible at times. And trying to find recipes that tick all of these boxes can be another add-on to your already busy daily schedule.

When all-in-one, or thermo, cooking devices first came onto the market 15 years ago, no one was prepared for the immediate attraction and, soon after, the devotion customers would have to this new way of preparing and cooking food. There was a realisation that these machines could help make healthy meals with minimal mess and fuss, and they would save time and money in the process – it was nothing short of a winning combination.

There is now an array of brands available with varying price tags. Although the original machines were and are expensive, there are now some costing considerably less, giving many people the opportunity of owning one.

Once you start looking through the recipes in this book, you will begin to understand the capabilities of these all-in-one devices and see that they are way more than just a food processor. You could almost think of them as an extra set of hands in the kitchen.

Using a thermo appliance means that you are able to more easily cook and feed your family delicious whole foods every day. The set-and-check functionality of a thermo device gives you back your most valuable asset in everyday cooking – your time! Being able to cook items at consistent temperatures, without having to worry about constantly returning to the stove to stir to prevent sticking or a pot from boiling over, means that the mess and stress of preparing whole foods is drastically reduced.

If you're a first-time thermo appliance user, head straight to the Whole food basics section on page 11. In this chapter you will learn that by purchasing whole grains and raw nuts and seeds and then using your thermo appliance to turn these into fresh batches of flour, nut meals and nut or seed milks provides a far superior flavour and nutrient content than store-bought options. Plus by swapping your store-bought staples with the recipes in this cookbook you can take great comfort in knowing exactly what is going into every single recipe you prepare – no more nasties, such as additives, preservatives and refined sugars.

The chapters Break-the-fast, Soulful soups, Delicious mains and Simple sides are all jam-packed with healthy and mouthwatering recipes that the whole family will love. The Wholesome sweets and Drinks, smoothies and shakes chapters are loaded with essential nutrient-dense, fibre-filling and fruit flavours that will please the sweetest of sweet tooths.

I have always found that getting children involved in food preparation, particularly at dinnertime, is a great way for them to try new foods and also gain a keen appetite for the meal ahead. Along with your guidance, our thermo appliance makes this a fun and easy way for children to learn some basic cooking principles.

Embrace and enjoy everything that your new-found and time-saving thermo appliance is capable of. Get inspired by the healthy recipes and delicious world of whole food cooking that are within this cookbook. Be courageous and try something new. You will find many family favourites in this book that I guarantee you will keep coming back to, time and again.

TIPS ON USING A THERMO DEVICE

Here are some useful points to note if you are a thermo newbie.

- No two brands or batches of the same ingredients will give the same results. This is important to note as you will find that, depending on the freshness of certain whole foods, particularly whole grains, nuts and seeds, you will get differing results – especially when milling. My general rule of thumb for milling is, after you have milled your batch for the time given in the recipe, feel the texture of the flour or meal between two fingers. If there is any grittiness simply mill again for 1 minute at the specified speed until you have a beautifully soft-feeling flour. The smoothness of the milled ingredients will impact how your baking goods turn out.
- It is assumed that all meat, poultry and especially seafood will be fresh, not frozen and thawed. You will find that a lot more liquid will be released from frozen items that have been thawed, especially prawns (shrimp). Always purchase fresh items for best results.

- What you place in your thermo appliance is what you get out of it. If you use fresh whole foods in season, the flavour will be at its peak and your dishes will taste better – plus the price will be lower.
- Where budget and time allow, purchase locally and organically farmed and produced items. Visiting farmers' markets and farm gates are much cheaper options than your regular supermarket shop.

SEAFOOD

Always purchase the listed sustainable seafood options in the ingredients list in the recipes of this cookbook to make sure you are doing your part in keeping our waters safe from overfishing.

SEASONING

You will notice that I don't say where to season your food in this cookbook, simply because everyone has their own taste requirements. Also, when using a thermo appliance, all of the flavour and nutrients are locked into the mixer bowl so you will find that the flavours of your dishes will be more intense than usual, which is fabulous!

At home I always place Murray River pink sea salt and a pepper grinder filled with tri-coloured peppercorn on the table at mealtimes for anyone who may need to add more seasoning. However, I find that by simply cooking with an abundance of fresh aromatic herbs or dried herbs and spices, flavouring with fresh lemon or lime or by adding either a Winter or Summer stock 'cube' (see pages 34–5) when cooking, no extra seasoning is needed.

SPECIAL DIETS

If you or a family member have a special eating requirement, then this book has you covered. Every recipe is tagged to indicate whether it is dairy-free, gluten-free, nut-free, paleo, vegan or vegetarian.

FOOD SAFETY

Be sure to read thoroughly the disclaimer on page 240 for safety guidelines.

DIETARY TAGS

DAIRY-FREE
GLUTEN-FREE
NUT-FREE
PALEO
VEGAN
VEGETARIAN

whole food

basics

FRESH RICOTTA

I defy anyone to be able to wait for this to cool before tasting it. Fresh home-made ricotta is so delicate and delicious, and children really love seeing how it gets 'created'. Don't forget to keep the whey, as this is really wonderful added to smoothies and shakes, sweet baking recipes or even scrambled eggs.

MAKES APPROXIMATELY 250 G (9 OZ/1 CUP)

Preparation time 10 minutes
Cooking time 2 minutes + standing

1 litre (35 fl oz/4 cups) unhomogenised organic full-cream (whole) milk
1 tablespoon apple cider vinegar

Insert the whisk attachment into the mixer bowl. Heat the milk for **10 min/80°C/speed 2**. Add the vinegar. Mix for **1 min/reverse stir/ speed 1**. Stand the milk mixture in the mixer bowl for 2 minutes to allow the curd to settle.

Meanwhile, set a fine-mesh sieve over a deep bowl and line the sieve with muslin (cheesecloth).

Carefully pour the milk mixture into the lined sieve. Stand for 30 minutes to drain, making sure the base of the sieve does not touch the whey in the bowl.

Use the ricotta immediately or chill it in an airtight container for up to 3 days. Use the whey immediately or chill it in an airtight container for up to 3 days.

GLUTEN-FREE | NUT-FREE | VEGETARIAN

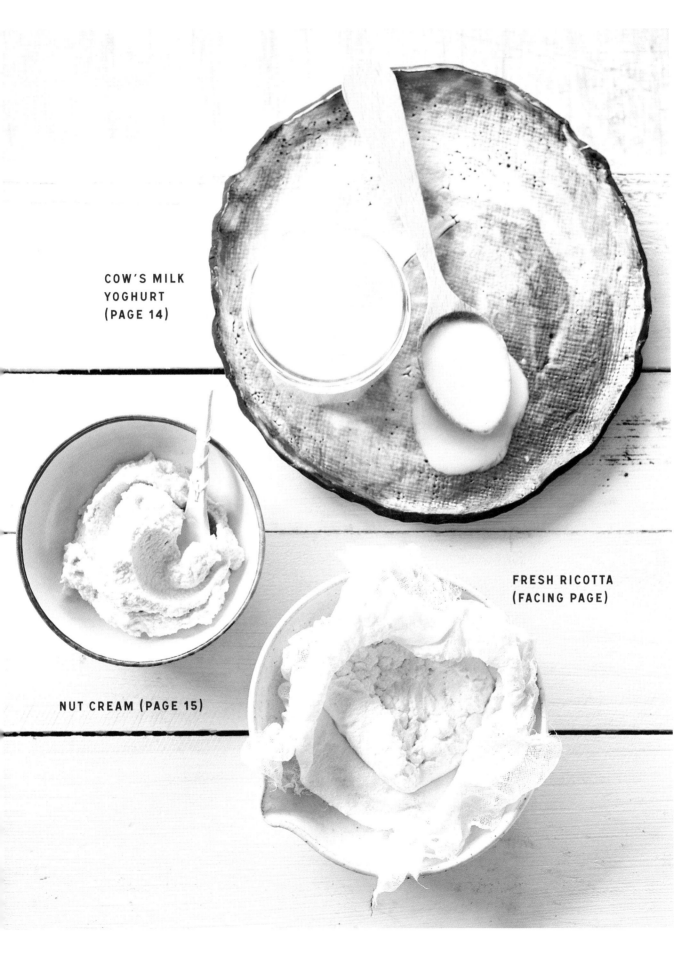

COW'S MILK
YOGHURT
(PAGE 14)

FRESH RICOTTA
(FACING PAGE)

NUT CREAM (PAGE 15)

COW'S MILK YOGHURT

The beauty of making your own yoghurt is that you know there are no added nasties or excess sugar, and you can use it for sweet or savoury dishes. It's so, so easy to make your own yoghurt at home using your mixer – it does all the hard work of temperature setting, which means you can simply walk away and come back when needed. Be sure to always reserve a good 125 g (4½ oz/½ cup) of the yoghurt you make to start off your next batch. It's safe to say you can do this about four to six times before having to start with another store-bought tub of yoghurt. Note that this is a soft-set yoghurt.

MAKES 4 X 250 ML (9 FL OZ/1 CUP) JARS
Preparation time 5 minutes + chilling
Cooking time 45 minutes + cooling and standing

1 litre (35 fl oz/4 cups) unhomogenised organic full-cream (whole) cow's milk
200 g (7 oz) organic full-cream (whole) natural yoghurt

Cook the milk for **25 min/90°C/speed 3**. Leave to cool in the mixer bowl for 1¼ hours (or until the mixture reaches 37°C). Discard any skin that has formed on top.

Insert the whisk attachment. Whisk a small amount of the cooled milk with the yoghurt until smooth. Pour this mixture back into the remaining milk in the mixer bowl. Cook for **20 min/37°C/speed 2**.

Pour the yoghurt mixture into four 250 ml (9 fl oz/1 cup) sterilised glass jars (see Note page 52) with airtight lids. Seal. Wrap each jar in a thick tea towel (dish towel). Place in a portable food cooler, add boiling water to a depth of about 5 cm (2 inches) and close the lid. Stand for 7 hours or overnight. Chill before serving. The yoghurt will keep chilled in the sealed jars for up to 4 weeks.

See photograph on page 13.

GLUTEN-FREE | NUT-FREE | VEGETARIAN

NUT CREAM

This is the perfect vegan alternative to cow's milk cream. With a super creamy and silky texture, you can use it for savoury or sweet dishes. Use as is for any savoury dish or add a generous splash of lemon juice to make it a 'soured' cream. Or, you can add some pure vanilla and either pure maple syrup or raw honey to taste and use the cream to spread over or dollop on any sweet dish.

MAKES 310 ML (10¾ FL OZ/1¼ CUPS)

Preparation time 5 minutes + standing

100 g (3½ oz) raw cashew nuts
1½ teaspoons sea salt
100 g (3½ oz) raw macadamia nuts

Place the cashew nuts and 1 teaspoon of the salt in a large bowl and cover with cold tap water. Stand for 6 hours. Drain and rinse in cold running water. Drain again.

Blend the cashew nuts, macadamia nuts, 125 ml (4 fl oz/½ cup) water and the remaining salt for **1 min/speed 8**. Blend again for **1 min/speed 8**.

Use the cream immediately or chill it in an airtight container for up to 5 days.

See photograph on page 13.

DAIRY-FREE | GLUTEN-FREE | PALEO | VEGAN | VEGETARIAN

NOTE

You can easily make a sweeter version of this nut cream by adding 2 tablespoons raw honey to the mixture before blending.

VANILLA PEPITA MILK

This milk is a great addition to any sweet baking, smoothies or shakes. I especially love adding some to my tea and coffee in the afternoon. Just always give the milk a good shake before using as there will be some sediment in the base of the container.

MAKES APPROXIMATELY 900 ML (31 FL OZ)

Preparation time 5 minutes
Cooking time 5 minutes + cooling

120 g (4¼ oz) pepitas (pumpkin seeds)
1 vanilla bean, split lengthways, seeds scraped
1 small pinch ground cinnamon
1 pinch sea salt

Mill the pepitas for **30 sec/speed 10**. Scrape down the side of the bowl.

Add the vanilla, cinnamon, salt and 1 litre (35 fl oz/4 cups) water. Cook for **5 min/60°C/speed 4**. Leave to cool in the mixer bowl.

Blend for **20 sec/speed 6**.

Line a fine-mesh sieve with some muslin (cheesecloth). Strain the mixture through the muslin into a jar or resealable jug.

Use the milk immediately or seal the jar and chill for up to 5 days.

See photograph on pages 18–19.

DAIRY-FREE | GLUTEN-FREE | NUT-FREE | PALEO | VEGAN | VEGETARIAN

BROWN RICE MILK

Home-made rice milk is so creamy and delicious and is great added to breakfast dishes such as Steel-cut oats (page 42) or Stewed-fruit bircher (page 43). It trumps store-bought varieties and will save you buckets of money. You can add a few teaspoons of pure maple syrup to the mixture if you like.

MAKES APPROXIMATELY 900 ML (31 FL OZ)

Preparation time 5 minutes
Cooking time 5 minutes + cooling

100 g (3½ oz/½ cup) brown basmati rice
1 tablespoon coconut oil
1 pinch sea salt

Mill the rice for **1 min/speed 10**. Scrape down the side of the bowl.

Add the coconut oil, sea salt and 1 litre (35 fl oz/4 cups) water. Cook for **5 min/60°C/speed 4**. Leave to cool in the mixer bowl.

Blend for **20 sec/speed 6**.

Line a fine-mesh sieve with some muslin (cheesecloth). Strain the mixture through the muslin into a jar or resealable jug.

Use the milk immediately or seal the jar and chill for up to 1 week.

See photograph on pages 18–19.

DAIRY-FREE | GLUTEN-FREE | NUT-FREE | VEGAN | VEGETARIAN

COCONUT MILK

This never lasts long in my house and is a perfect addition to all forms of cooking – from breakfasts, soups and drinks to curries and sweets. My favourite use, though, is blending the finished milk with frozen fruit for a dairy-free 'nice-cream', or heating it gently before stirring through some Turmeric paste (page 33) to taste.

MAKES APPROXIMATELY 625 ML (21½ FL OZ/2½ CUPS)
Preparation time 5 minutes
Cooking time 5 minutes + cooling

150 g (5½ oz) coconut flakes

Mill the coconut for **10 sec/speed 9**. Scrape down the side of the bowl.

Add 500 ml (17 fl oz/2 cups) water. Cook for **5 min/60°C/speed 4**. Leave to cool in the mixer bowl.

Blend for **30 sec/speed 9**. Scrape down the side of the bowl. Blend for **30 sec/speed 9**.

Transfer the mixture to a jar or resealable jug.

Use the milk immediately or seal the jar and chill for up to 1 week.

NOTE
You can strain the coconut milk through a fine-mesh sieve if you like, for a silky smooth milk.

See photograph on pages 18–19.

DAIRY-FREE | GLUTEN-FREE | NUT-FREE | PALEO | VEGAN | VEGETARIAN

COCONUT CREAM

This is so much better than store-bought tinned coconut cream. Your mixture will also thicken the longer it is in the fridge. After a few days of chilling, transfer the very thick top layer of the cream to a bowl and use a balloon whisk to whisk it into soft peaks and then use in place of whipped cream on your sweet treats, or to top your warming drinks in the cooler months, or iced drinks in the warmer months. Add a bit of pure vanilla and pure maple syrup for added flavour.

MAKES 875 ML (30 FL OZ/3½ CUPS)
Preparation time 5 minutes
Cooking time 5 minutes + cooling

300 g (10½ oz) coconut flakes

Mill the coconut for **30 sec/speed 9**. Scrape down the side of the bowl.

Add 625 ml (21½ fl oz/2½ cups) water. Cook for **5 min/60°C/speed 4**. Leave to cool in the mixer bowl.

Blend for **30 sec/speed 9**. Scrape down the side of the bowl. Blend for **30 sec/speed 9**.

Transfer the mixture to a jar or resealable jug.

Use the cream immediately or seal the jar and chill for up to 1 week.

NOTE
You can strain the coconut cream through a fine-mesh sieve if you like, for a silky smooth cream.

See photograph on pages 18–19.

DAIRY-FREE | GLUTEN-FREE | NUT-FREE | PALEO | VEGAN | VEGETARIAN

BROWN RICE
MILK (PAGE 16)

COCONUT CREAM
(PAGE 17)

VANILLA PEPITA MILK
(PAGE 16)

COCONUT MILK
(PAGE 17)

EVERYDAY SPREADABLE BUTTER

Once you make your own butter you will never go back –
and it goes without saying that you can add any flavours to
this delicious spread, both savoury or sweet. I usually have a
few different butters on the go as well as this basic spreadable
version: a sea salt and garlic butter can be used for everyday
savoury cooking; a mixed herb butter for adding at the end
of dishes such as soups, stews, mashes and purées; and a
sweet one with pure maple syrup, lemon juice and ground
cinnamon for topping our Sunday pancakes.

MAKES 250 G (9 OZ/1 CUP)
Preparation time 5 minutes

600 ml (21 fl oz) organic thin (pouring/whipping) cream
1 litre (35 fl oz/4 cups) chilled water
60 ml (2 fl oz/¼ cup) macadamia oil

Insert the whisk attachment into the mixer bowl. Add the cream.
Whisk for **2 min/speed 4**. Check to see if the solids have separated
from the whey. If not, then whisk for **30 sec intervals/speed 4** until
the solids have separated from the whey.

Remove the whisk attachment. Strain the whey from the mixer bowl
into a jug and reserve. Leave the butter solids in the mixer bowl.

Add half the chilled water to the solids in the mixer bowl. Mix for
10 sec/speed 4. Strain through a fine-mesh sieve and discard the
liquid from the mixer bowl.

Add the remaining chilled water to the solids in the mixer bowl. Mix
for **10 sec/speed 4**. Strain and discard the liquid from the mixer bowl.

Add the oil and 60 ml (2 fl oz/¼ cup) of the reserved whey to the solids
in the mixer bowl. Mix for **15 sec/speed 4**.

Use the butter immediately or chill it in an airtight container for up to
2 weeks.

GLUTEN-FREE | VEGETARIAN

GARLIC FRYING OIL

I tend to make this when I have all those rogue cloves of garlic rolling around in my vegetable crisper – it's a great way to use them up, plus it's also wonderful having an oil on hand that can add instant flavour to any savoury recipe. Coconut oil has a high smoking point, meaning that you can cook with it at high temperatures, such as when stir-frying, high-heat pan-frying and barbecuing.

MAKES 300 ML (10½ FL OZ)
Preparation time 5 minutes
Cooking time 5 minutes + cooling

6 unpeeled garlic cloves
300 ml (10½ fl oz) coconut oil

Chop the garlic for **5 sec/reverse stir/speed 4**. Discard the skins. Chop the garlic for a further **5 sec/speed 4**. Scrape down the side of the bowl.

Add the oil, reserving the jar it came in, or set aside a 300 ml (10½ fl oz) jar or container. Cook for **5 minutes/90°C/speed 1**. Leave to cool in the mixer bowl.

Strain the oil through a fine-mesh sieve into the jar or container.

Use the oil immediately or seal it and chill it for up to 2 months.

DAIRY-FREE | GLUTEN-FREE | NUT-FREE | PALEO | VEGAN | VEGETARIAN

MACADAMIA PASTRY

This delicate, almost shortbread-like pastry offers a different soft and crumbly texture from standard pastry. The use of macadamia nuts in this pastry makes it great for both savoury and sweet baking — use it to line tart (flan) tins or pie plates, or to top savoury or sweet pies. Sometimes if I feel like being a bit fancy (and I can find the tool in my utensil drawer) I will use a pastry cutter to run around the edge of the pastry to neaten the ends before baking.

MAKES 545 G (1 LB 3 OZ)

Preparation time 5 minutes

210 g (7½ oz/1 cup) tapioca pearls
200 g (7 oz) raw macadamia nuts
½ teaspoon sea salt flakes
90 g (3¼ oz) chilled butter, chopped
1 chilled egg

Mill the tapioca for **1 min/speed 10**. Scrape down the side of the bowl. Add the macadamia nuts and mill for **3 sec/speed 9**. Add the salt, butter and the egg. Mix for **5 sec/speed 4**. Scrape down the side of the bowl. Mix again for **5 sec/speed 4**.

Tip the mixture out onto some plastic wrap and bring the dough together to form a soft disc. Use the pastry as needed or chill it for up to 3 days.

GLUTEN-FREE | PALEO | VEGETARIAN

NOTE

If you like the look of a darker pastry shell when cooked, dry-roast your macadamia nuts for 10–12 minutes in a 180°C (350°F) oven/ 160°C (315°F) fan-forced oven until golden, then cool before milling.

LEMON AND LIME SYRUP

There are so many uses for this zingy syrup. My favourites are: pouring some over crushed ice and topping with sparkling water; brushing a little over a freshly baked, warm vanilla cake; or adding more water and making iceblocks (popsicles/ ice lollies) for the children.

MAKES APPROXIMATELY 500 ML (17 FL OZ/2 CUPS)
Preparation time 5 minutes
Cooking time 10 minutes + cooling

4 lemons, zest finely grated, white pith removed, chopped and seeded
4 limes, zest finely grated, white pith removed, chopped and seeded
125 ml (4 fl oz/½ cup) raw honey

Blend the lemon and lime flesh for **10 sec/speed 7**. Scrape down the side of the bowl. Blend again for **10 sec/speed 5**. Scrape down the side of the bowl.

Add the honey and 375 ml (13 fl oz/1½ cups) water. Cook for **10 min/ 120°C/speed 1**. Leave to cool in the mixer bowl. Blend for **30 sec/speed 9**.

Stir through the lemon and lime zest. Use immediately or chill in an airtight glass jar for up to 2 weeks.

DAIRY-FREE | GLUTEN-FREE | NUT-FREE | PALEO | VEGETARIAN

SUPER-GREENS
PESTO (FACING PAGE)

AVO MAYO
(PAGE 26)

SUPER-GREENS PESTO

This is one of the easiest ways of getting all the important nutrients from these super-greens into your family's diet without anyone knowing.

MAKES 340 G (12 OZ/1⅓ CUPS)

Preparation time 5 minutes

80 g (2¾ oz/½ cup) pine nuts
1 garlic clove
1 large handful basil leaves
1 large handful baby rocket (arugula)
1 large handful baby English spinach leaves
1 large kale leaf, stem removed, torn
170 ml (5½ fl oz/⅔ cup) avocado oil
finely grated zest and juice of 1 lemon

Blend all the ingredients for **20 sec/speed 8**. Scrape down the side of the bowl. Blend again for **10 sec/speed 8**.

Use the pesto immediately or chill it in an airtight container for up to 5 days.

DAIRY-FREE | GLUTEN-FREE | PALEO | VEGAN | VEGETARIAN

AVO MAYO

This highly nutritious, fruity-flavoured oil is bursting with monounsaturated fats and vitamin E, so it's a fantastic fat to add into your diet – your skin, hair and nails will thank you for it. Plus, check out my flavour variations below to see how many uses this baby has.

MAKES APPROXIMATELY 435 G (15½ OZ/1¾ CUPS)
Preparation time 5 minutes

1 egg
1 tablespoon lemon juice
1 teaspoon sea salt
¼ teaspoon ground white pepper
500 ml (17 fl oz/2 cups) avocado oil

Put the egg, lemon juice, salt and pepper in the mixer bowl and mix for **5 min/speed 4**, while very slowly pouring the oil through the mixer bowl lid. Continue until the mixture emulsifies.

Use the mayonnaise immediately or chill it in an airtight container for up to 1 week.

See photograph on page 24.

DAIRY-FREE | GLUTEN-FREE | NUT-FREE | PALEO | VEGETARIAN

TRY THESE FLAVOUR OPTIONS:

Tartare – *stir in 3 tablespoons Fermented chopped salad (page 29)*

Sweet chilli – *stir in 1 tablespoon pure maple syrup and 1 finely chopped long red chilli*

Seafood sauce – *stir in the finely grated zest and juice of ½ lemon, 1 tablespoon Tomato mix (page 28) and 2 tablespoons dill fronds*

Smoky – *stir in 2 teaspoons Tomato mix (page 28), 1 tablespoon chopped coriander (cilantro) and 2 teaspoons smoked paprika.*

ESPRESSO BARBECUE SAUCE

I can't take credit for this sauce recipe – it's one that my husband created for Valentine's Day way back when. All I have done is convert it to a much simpler method for the all-in-one mixer. This sauce really is delicious on all kinds of protein, apart from delicate seafood – it rocks as a dipper for barbecued prawns (shrimp), though. Our favourite use is spreading it over slow-cooked beef or pork ribs before grilling.

MAKES APPROXIMATELY 350 G (12 OZ/3 CUPS)

Preparation time 10 minutes
Cooking time 40 minutes + cooling

500 g (1 lb 2 oz) tomatoes, cored and quartered
1 red onion, peeled and quartered
2 red capsicums (peppers), cut into 8
6 garlic cloves
1 long red chilli, cut into 3
1 teaspoon smoked paprika
1 rosemary sprig, leaves stripped
1 tablespoon yellow mustard seeds
125 ml (4 fl oz/½ cup) espresso coffee
125 ml (4 fl oz/½ cup) pure maple syrup
80 ml (2½ fl oz/⅓ cup) apple cider vinegar

Blend all the ingredients for **20 sec/speed 6**. Scrape down the side of the bowl.

Attach the simmering basket, instead of the measuring cup, to the mixer bowl lid. Cook for **40 min/120°C/speed 2**.

Pour the hot mixture into some warm sterilised glass jars (see Note page 52) with airtight lids. Seal. Turn the jars upside down onto a doubled over tea towel (dish towel) and leave to cool.

Store the sauce out of direct sunlight for up to 3 months. Once opened, chill it for up to 1 month or freeze for up to 6 months.

DAIRY-FREE | GLUTEN-FREE | NUT-FREE | PALEO | VEGAN | VEGETARIAN

NOTE
If you would like a smoother sauce, simply blend the cooled mixture for 30 sec/speed 9.

TOMATO MIX

This multipurpose tomato recipe is great for using as a tomato sauce (ketchup) and as a tomato paste (concentrated purée). If you purée 125 ml (4 fl oz/½ cup) of the mixture with an additional 500 g (1 lb 2 oz) cored and quartered tomatoes, you will have a delicious tomato pasta sauce (passata). I make the recipe several times over the summer months when tomatoes are at their sweetest and most affordable.

MAKES 410 G (14½ OZ/3½ CUPS)

Preparation time 10 minutes
Cooking time 40 minutes + cooling

1 kg (2 lb 4 oz) tomatoes, cored and quartered
1 red onion, peeled and quartered
2 garlic cloves
1 teaspoon dried mixed herbs
1 teaspoon sweet paprika
2 teaspoons sea salt
½ teaspoon ground white pepper
2 tablespoons apple cider vinegar
60 ml (2 fl oz/¼ cup) pure maple syrup

Blend all the ingredients for **1 min/speed 6**. Scrape down the side of the bowl.

Attach the simmering basket, instead of the measuring cup, to the mixer bowl lid. Cook for **40 min/120°C/speed 2**.

Pour the hot mixture into some warm, sterilised glass jars (see Note page 52) with airtight lids. Seal. Turn the jars upside down onto a doubled over tea towel (dish towel) and leave to cool.

Store the tomato mix out of direct sunlight for up to 3 months. Once opened, chill it for up to 1 month. You can also freeze it in 125 g (4½ oz/ ½ cup) portions for up to 6 months.

DAIRY-FREE | GLUTEN-FREE | NUT-FREE | PALEO | VEGAN | VEGETARIAN

NOTE
Depending on the ripeness of your tomatoes and how juicy they are, you may need to cook them for a further 5–10 minutes. Just check the mix after cooking and if it looks watery continue to cook until slightly thickened – you want the mix to be of a passata (puréed tomatoes) consistency. If you would like a smoother mix, simply blend the cooled mixture for 30 sec/speed 9.

FERMENTED CHOPPED SALAD

Eating fermented foods is so great for your gut health, especially if you have digestive issues. Having good gut health will boost your immunity and your mood. Adding a couple of spoonfuls of this deliciously tangy accompaniment to your meals every day will help in maintaining levels of live 'good' bacteria in your system.

MAKES 1 KG (2 LB 4 OZ/5 CUPS)

Preparation time 10 minutes + standing

1 red onion, peeled and quartered
200 g (7 oz) red cabbage, cut into 3 cm (1¼ inch) pieces
200 g (7 oz) green cabbage, cut into 3 cm (1¼ inch) pieces
2 carrots, cut into 4
200 g (7 oz) broccoli, cut into florets
200 g (7 oz) cauliflower, cut into florets
1 Lebanese (short) cucumber, cut into 3
2 tablespoons sea salt

Chop the onion, cabbage and carrot for **3 sec/speed 7**. Transfer to a large bowl.

Chop the broccoli and cauliflower for **3 sec/speed 7**. Add to the bowl with the cabbage mixture.

Chop the cucumber and salt for **3 sec/speed 5** and add to the bowl with the other vegetables. Using your hands, massage the mixture together until you see the vegetables start to release their natural juices.

Transfer the mixture to a sterilised glass jar (see Note page 52) with an airtight lid. Place a left-over cabbage leaf on top, if desired, and press the mixture down as firmly as possible to pack the vegetables tightly and release more liquid from the mixture.

Make sure the vegetables are covered by the liquid, then seal the jar. (You can add some of the left-over outer leaves of the cabbage to submerge the vegetables in the liquid.) Stand the salad out of direct sunlight for 3–5 days, depending on how tart you like your fermented salad to be.

Use the salad immediately or chill it until ready to serve. Once opened, chill it for up to 1 month.

See photograph on page 31.

DAIRY-FREE | GLUTEN-FREE NUT-FREE | PALEO | VEGAN | VEGETARIAN

PEAR AND POMEGRANATE CHUTNEY

This delicious autumn chutney is a terrific all-rounder. Spread it over your toasties, use it as a glaze over roast lamb or add a dollop on the side of your favourite curry. Get yourself organised and make a few batches as the chutney will keep, unopened and stored out of direct sunlight, for up to 6 months. If you can be patient, try to leave the chutney for 2–3 weeks before opening to allow the flavours to really develop.

MAKES 890 G (1 LB 15 OZ)

Preparation time 10 minutes
Cooking time 45 minutes + cooling

3 cm (1¼ inch) piece fresh ginger, peeled and halved
1 long red chilli, cut into 3
1 brown onion, peeled and quartered
1 green apple, quartered and cored
3 large (800 g/1 lb 12 oz) green pears, quartered and cored
250 ml (9 fl oz/1 cup) apple cider vinegar
250 ml (9 fl oz/1 cup) pure maple syrup
1 cinnamon stick
4 whole cloves
seeds of 1 small pomegranate (see Note)

Chop the ginger, chilli and onion for **4 sec/speed 5**. Scrape down the side of the bowl.

Add the apple and pear. Chop for **5 sec/speed 5**. Scrape down the side of the bowl. Add the vinegar, maple syrup, cinnamon stick and cloves.

Attach the simmering basket, instead of the measuring cup, to the mixer bowl lid. Cook for **45 min/100°C/reverse stir/speed 1**. Remove the cinnamon stick (or you can add it to the top of the jar).

Add the pomegranate seeds. Stir for **30 sec/reverse stir/speed 1**.

Pour the hot mixture into some warm sterilised glass jars (see Note page 52) with airtight lids. Seal. Turn the jars upside down onto a doubled over tea towel (dish towel) and leave to cool.

Store the chutney out of direct sunlight for up to 6 months. Once opened, chill for up to 1 month.

DAIRY-FREE | GLUTEN-FREE | NUT-FREE | VEGAN | VEGETARIAN

NOTE
You can remove the pomegranate seeds easily by halving the fruit and then tapping the top of the fruit with a rolling pin.

FERMENTED
CHOPPED SALAD
(PAGE 29)

PEAR AND
POMEGRANATE
CHUTNEY
(FACING PAGE)

ASIAN PASTE

I just love this recipe – it's my favourite go-to 'flavour booster' for all of my Asian cooking and keeps so well in the fridge, too. For Thai-inspired meals I will add kaffir lime and coriander (cilantro) leaves; for Japanese dishes I will add spring onion (scallion) and miso paste; and for a Chinese twist I will add sesame oil and tamari (gluten-free soy sauce).

MAKES 200 G (7 OZ/1½ CUPS)

Preparation time 10 minutes
Cooking time 5 minutes

2 tablespoons dried chilli flakes
1 red onion, peeled and quartered
4 garlic cloves
2 lemongrass stalks, trimmed and cut into
   3 cm (1¼ inch) lengths, bruised
4 cm (1½ inch) piece fresh ginger, peeled
1 tablespoon ground coriander
1 tablespoon ground cumin

Cook the chilli and 125 ml (4 fl oz/½ cup) water for **5 min/120°C/reverse stir/speed 1**.

Add all the remaining ingredients. Mix for **20 sec/speed 7**. Scrape down the side of the bowl. Mix again for **20 sec/speed 7**.

Transfer the paste to a sterilised glass jar (see Note page 52). Use immediately or chill it for up to 6 months.

DAIRY-FREE | GLUTEN-FREE | NUT-FREE | PALEO | VEGAN | VEGETARIAN

TURMERIC PASTE

This is a powerful anti-inflammatory, anti-fungal paste, which can be easily added into your daily life. I add a couple of teaspoons to some warm nut milk for a lovely drink either in the morning or before bed. Or I mix it with avocado oil and use it as a dressing on salads. You can also add a few spoonfuls to your serving of soup or curry or add a generous spoonful to a smoothie.

MAKES APPROXIMATELY 110 G (3¾ OZ)

Preparation time 5 minutes
Cooking time 10 minutes + cooling

1 teaspoon black peppercorns
6 cm (2½ inch) piece fresh turmeric, peeled and halved
50 g (1¾ oz/⅓ cup) ground turmeric
80 ml (2½ fl oz/⅓ cup) coconut oil
60 ml (2 fl oz/¼ cup) raw honey

Mill the peppercorns for **30 sec/speed 9**. Scrape down the side of the bowl. Transfer to a bowl and set aside.

Add the fresh turmeric and chop for **30 sec/speed 9**. Scrape down the side of the bowl.

Add the ground turmeric and 250 ml (9 fl oz/1 cup) water. Cook for **10 min/90°C/speed 2**.

Add the coconut oil and the reserved milled peppercorns. Mix for **10 sec/speed 4**. Leave to cool in the mixer bowl.

Add the honey and mix for **10 sec/speed 4**. Transfer the turmeric paste to a sterilised glass jar (see Note page 52), seal and chill for up to 2 weeks.

DAIRY-FREE | GLUTEN-FREE | NUT-FREE | PALEO | VEGETARIAN

SUMMER STOCK 'CUBES'

All the sweet-tasting, light flavours of the warmer months are added to this recipe – but, by all means, simply add whatever vegetables you have in your fridge at the time. There's no need to thaw these stock cubes – simply add them from the freezer straight to your mixer when cooking.

MAKES APPROXIMATELY 70 CUBES

Preparation time 10 minutes
Cooking time 15 minutes + freezing

2 red onions, peeled and quartered
4 carrots, cut into 3
4 celery stalks, cut into 4 cm (1½ inch) lengths
2 garlic cloves
2 red capsicums (peppers), seeded and cut into 8
2 zucchini (courgettes), cut into 3
2 tomatoes, cored and quartered
1 large handful basil leaves
1 large handful flat-leaf (Italian) parsley leaves
3 tablespoons thyme leaves
1 tablespoon sea salt
2 tablespoons water

Line four large baking trays with baking paper.

Chop all the ingredients for **30 sec/speed 7**. Scrape down the side of the bowl.

Cook for **15 min/120°C/speed 1**.

Blend for **1 min/speed 6**. Place level tablespoonfuls of the mixture onto the prepared trays in a single layer. Freeze for 1 hour or until frozen firm.

To store, layer the stock cubes between sheets of baking paper in an airtight container or resealable food storage bags. They will keep frozen for up to 6 months.

DAIRY-FREE | GLUTEN-FREE | NUT-FREE | PALEO | VEGAN | VEGETARIAN

NOTE
If short on time (or baking trays), simply make two large trays of stock cubes then freeze the remaining stock mixture in 125 ml (4 fl oz/½ cup) measures and place them in resealable food storage bags. That way you can pull out a batch and thaw as needed.

WINTER STOCK 'CUBES'

All the hearty flavours of the cooler months are added to this recipe – all my favourite winter vegies. Feel free to add any other root vegetables that are in season, but steer clear of using potatoes, as these don't freeze well.

MAKES APPROXIMATELY 60 CUBES
Preparation time 10 minutes
Cooking time 15 minutes + freezing

2 leeks, trimmed and cut into 3 cm (1¼ inch) lengths
4 carrots, cut into 3
4 celery stalks, cut into 4 cm (1½ inch) lengths
2 garlic cloves
2 baby fennel bulbs, cut into 4
200 g (7 oz) celeriac, peeled and cut into
    3 cm (1¼ inch) pieces
200 g (7 oz) pumpkin, peeled, seeded and cut into
    3 cm (1¼ inch) pieces
3 tablespoons rosemary leaves
3 tablespoons French tarragon leaves
1 handful sage leaves
1 tablespoon sea salt
2 tablespoons water

Line four large baking trays with baking paper.

Chop all the ingredients for **30 sec/speed 5**. Scrape down the side of the bowl.

Cook for **15 min/120°C/speed 1**.

Blend for **1 min/speed 6**. Place level tablespoonfuls of the mixture onto the prepared trays in a single layer. Freeze for 1 hour or until frozen firm.

To store, layer the stock cubes between sheets of baking paper in an airtight container or resealable food storage bags. They will keep frozen for up to 6 months.

DAIRY-FREE | GLUTEN-FREE | NUT-FREE | PALEO | VEGAN | VEGETARIAN

NOTE

If short on time (or baking trays), simply make two large trays of stock cubes then freeze the remaining stock mixture in 125 ml (4 fl oz/½ cup) measures and place them in resealable food storage bags. That way you can pull out a batch and thaw as needed.

PREPARING AND COOKING DRIED BEANS AND PULSES

Purchasing and cooking your own dried beans and pulses will save you so much money. With a little planning ahead you can have an array of delicious beans and pulses on hand whenever needed. Since it has been found that there is a potentially harmful chemical, BPA, in the lining of all tinned products, it is also much safer for your and your family's health to cook these little gems from scratch. Low in fat, so very high in fibre and the perfect protein food, give them a try with my simple instructions.

SOAKING

Please note, you will not need to pre-soak pulses such as lentils and split peas as these are quick-cooking — meaning they will soften on cooking from anywhere between 20 and 45 minutes.

Soaking dried beans improves their digestibility and reduces the cooking time. Please allow at least 1 litre (35 fl oz/4 cups) of water per 1 cup of dried beans used. Place them in a large bowl, covered with the required water, then cover them with a clean tea towel (dish towel) and stand overnight (or a minimum of 6 hours) out of direct sunlight and away from any heat source. Drain well, rinsing, picking over and discarding any that are dark coloured.

COOKING

Depending on the age of your dried beans and pulses, you may find that the cooking time will need to be increased. Do this in 10-minute increments, making sure there is enough water in the mixer bowl each time. You want the beans and pulses to be al dente, as they will generally get cooked or reheated again in your recipe.

Referring to the table below, place your soaked, rinsed and drained beans into your mixer bowl. Add the required water plus two pieces of kombu (dried seaweed, available from Asian grocers) – this will help reduce the gas-producing properties of the beans. If you are unable to find kombu you can use a teaspoon each of fennel seeds and cumin seeds plus a slice of peeled fresh ginger to help with the same issue. Sometimes I add all these. Cook as directed, then use or cool before chilling in an airtight container for up to 3 days or freezing in 1 cup portions in resealable food storage bags for up to 6 months. Please don't add any salt or lemon juice to your beans when cooking as this can prevent them from softening.

BEAN/PULSE	SOAKING	WATER FOR COOKING	APPROX. COOKING TIME (SEE NOTE)	APPROX. COOKED WEIGHT
200 g (7 oz) Dried chickpeas	Yes – in 1 litre (35 fl oz/4 cups) water	1 litre (35 fl oz/ 4 cups) water	60 min/100°C/ reverse stir/ speed 2	425 g (15 oz/ 2½ cups)
200 g (7 oz) Dried black beans	Yes – in 1 litre (35 fl oz/4 cups) water	1 litre (35 fl oz/ 4 cups)	60 min/100°C/ reverse stir/ speed 2	425 g (15 oz/ 2½ cups)
200 g (7 oz) Dried red kidney beans	Yes – in 1 litre (35 fl oz/4 cups) water	1 litre (35 fl oz/ 4 cups)	60 min/100°C/ reverse stir/ speed 2	425 g (15 oz/ 2½ cups)
200 g (7 oz) Dried French blue-green lentils	No	1 litre (35 fl oz/ 4 cups)	40 min/100°C/ reverse stir/ speed 2	425 g (15 oz/ 2½ cups)

break-the-fast

MAPLE PECAN TOASTED MUESLI

You can save LOADS of money on your grocery bill if you simply ditch any form of packaged muesli product from your kitchen cupboard. This version rocks in flavour and texture – make a couple of batches at a time as it stores well. It's a good little topper for your morning smoothie or night-time 'nice-cream' treat. Serve it swimming in your favourite milk or with a generous dollop of Cow's milk yoghurt (page 14) topped with your favourite seasonal fresh fruit.

MAKES APPROXIMATELY 900 G (2 LB/6 CUPS)

Preparation time 5 minutes
Cooking time 26 minutes + cooling

125 g (4½ oz) unsalted butter, chopped
440 g (15½ oz) rolled (porridge) oats
50 g (1¾ oz/½ cup) pecans
75 g (2¾ oz/½ cup) pepitas (pumpkin seeds)
80 ml (2½ fl oz/⅓ cup) pure maple syrup
milk of choice, to serve

Preheat the oven to 200°C (400°F)/180°C (350°F) fan-forced. Line a large baking tray with baking paper.

Melt the butter for **1 min/120°C/speed 1**. Add all the remaining ingredients. Chop for **5 sec/speed 5**.

Transfer the oat mixture to the prepared tray. Using your fingertips, gently spread the mixture out evenly over the tray (there should be some crumbly bits and some macadamia-sized clumps).

Bake the mixture for 25 minutes, carefully turning twice during cooking, or until golden and crisp. Leave to cool on the tray.

Eat the muesli immediately with your milk of choice, or store out of direct sunlight in an airtight container for up to 2 weeks.

VEGETARIAN

STEEL-CUT OATS

Don't be fooled, these oats just have a very fancy-sounding name, but they are totally mainstream – and by that I mean you can purchase steel-cut oats in large supermarkets. The thing about steel-cut oats is that they don't actually look like oats (as you probably know them) as they haven't been rolled, but have been coarsely chopped instead, giving them a look of smashed-up pieces of dark brown rice. They are this colour as they haven't been precooked and have the bran and germ all still intact. Therefore, this grain will keep you feeling fuller for so much longer than your regular rolled (porridge) oats will. I generally blend the cinnamon and nut mixture for the adults more coarsely and then blend the kids' serves much finer – my kids like to call this 'doughnut dust'.

SERVES 4

Preparation time 5 minutes
Cooking time 20 minutes

40 g (1½ oz/¼ cup) whole natural almonds
40 g (1½ oz/¼ cup) raw cashew nuts
2 tablespoons shelled pistachio nuts
1 teaspoon ground cinnamon
270 g (9½ oz/1½ cups) steel-cut oats
500 ml (17 fl oz/2 cups) milk of choice
raw honey, to serve

Chop the almonds, cashew nuts, pistachio nuts and cinnamon for **30 sec/speed 4**.

Transfer the nut mixture to a bowl. Add the oats, milk and 375 ml (13 fl oz/1½ cups) water to the mixer bowl. Cook for **20 min/100°C/ reverse stir/speed 1**.

Serve warm topped with the nut mixture and honey, to taste.

VEGETARIAN

STEWED-FRUIT BIRCHER

This is my favourite make-ahead brekkie. Both the bircher mixture and stewed fruit can be made the night before and simply mixed together before serving in the morning. Swap the rhubarb for an all-berry mix or pear or apple, so you can enjoy this dish year-round. I actually quite like this recipe in the cooler months – I simply serve the stewed fruit warm.

SERVES 4

Preparation time 10 minutes
Cooking time 10 minutes + chilling

200 g (7 oz/2 cups) rolled (porridge) oats
250 ml (9 fl oz/1 cup) milk of choice
250 ml (9 fl oz/1 cup) Cow's milk yoghurt (page 14)
1 bunch rhubarb stems, trimmed, washed and cut
   into 5 cm (2 inch) lengths
250 g (9 oz) small strawberries, hulled
2 tablespoons lemon juice
80 ml (2½ fl oz/⅓ cup) pure maple syrup
1 teaspoon ground cardamom

Chop the oats for **10 sec/speed 6**. Add the milk and yoghurt. Stir for **30 sec/speed 1**.

Transfer the mixture to a bowl, cover it, then chill overnight.

Add the rhubarb, strawberry, lemon juice, maple syrup and cardamom to the mixer bowl. Attach the simmering basket, instead of the measuring cup, to the mixer bowl lid. Cook for **10 min/100°C/reverse stir/speed 2**.

Use the fruit warm or chill in an airtight container overnight along with the bircher.

Divide the bircher among serving bowls and top with the stewed fruit, either warm or cool. Serve.

NUT-FREE | VEGETARIAN

NOTES

I find the cardamom works so beautifully with the rhubarb and strawberry, but it can easily be interchanged with either ground cinnamon, ground mixed (pumpkin pie) spice or ground ginger.

You will need half a lemon to yield 2 tablespoons juice.

CARROT SCONE

This is a cross between damper and a scone, which has to be served hot with lashings of butter and honey. Pop it on the table and cut it into wedges or just let everyone tear off sections as they need – it truly is delicious and won't last long. I have never made one of these and had leftovers...

SERVES 8

Preparation time 10 minutes
Cooking time 45 minutes

450 g (1 lb/2 cups) whole wheat grains (see Note)
2 carrots, cut into 3
100 g (3½ oz) chilled unsalted butter, chopped
2 teaspoons baking powder
1 teaspoon ground mixed (pumpkin pie) spice
1 egg
60 ml (2 fl oz/¼ cup) pure maple syrup
½ teaspoon pure vanilla extract
180 ml (6 fl oz/¾ cup) milk of choice
Everyday spreadable butter (page 20), to serve
raw honey, to serve

Preheat the oven to 180°C (350°F)/160°C (315°F) fan-forced. Line a large baking tray with baking paper.

Mill the wheat grains for **1 min/speed 10**.

Add the carrot and chop for **5 sec/speed 5**. Scrape down the side of the bowl.

Add the butter, baking powder and mixed spice. Mix for **5 sec/speed 5**. Scrape down the side of the bowl.

Add the egg, maple syrup, vanilla and milk. Knead for **4 min/dough mode**. The mixture will still look moist but will hold its shape when it's transferred to the baking tray.

Transfer the mixture to the prepared tray, gently shaping it into an 18 cm (7 inch) round. (The scone will spread during baking.)

Bake for 45 minutes or until cooked and golden. Serve the carrot scone immediately with butter and honey (or see suggestions left).

NUT-FREE | VEGETARIAN

SERVING SUGGESTIONS

Nut cream (page 15), Pear and pomegranate chutney (page 30), Spiced plum spread (page 52) or Strawberry spread (page 53).

NOTE

Whole wheat grains are readily available at health food stores, continental delis, greengrocers and online. They're cheaper if you buy them in bulk.

RICOTTA AND SPINACH MUFFINS

These are too tempting not to eat warm straight from the oven, or to stop at just one. They're packed with protein and travel and freeze well, plus they're equally delicious served as a warming afternoon snack.

MAKES 12

Preparation time 10 minutes
Cooking time 20 minutes + standing

225 g (8 oz/1 cup) whole wheat grains (see Note page 45)
100 g (3½ oz) butter, chopped
100 g (3½ oz) baby English spinach leaves
½ bunch chives, cut into 3 cm (1¼ inch) lengths
2 thyme sprigs, leaves stripped
2 teaspoons baking powder
2 eggs
230 g (8½ oz/1 cup) Fresh ricotta (page 12)

Preheat the oven to 200°C (400°F)/180°C (350°F) fan-forced. Line a 12-hole, 80 ml (2½ fl oz/⅓ cup) capacity muffin tin with paper cases.

Mill the wheat grains for **1 min/speed 9**. Transfer the milled wheat to a bowl.

Melt the butter for **1 min/100°C/speed 1**. Add the spinach, chives and thyme. Chop for **20 sec/speed 4**. Scrape down the side of the bowl.

Add the baking powder, eggs and milled wheat. Mix for **20 sec/speed 5**. Scrape down the side of the bowl. Add the ricotta. Mix for **5 sec/speed 4**.

Divide the ricotta mixture evenly among paper cases in the pan. Bake for 25 minutes or until cooked and golden. Leave to stand for 5 minutes in the tin. Serve the muffins warm or at room temperature.

NUT-FREE | VEGETARIAN

SERVING SUGGESTIONS

Dollop with either Tomato mix (page 28), Espresso barbecue sauce (page 27) or Pear and pomegranate chutney (page 30).

PAN WAFFLES

These gluten-free, paleo-friendly pan waffles are the fastest breakfast to prep and always a good way to use up those overripe bananas in the fruit bowl. You can change to a nut-free option also by swapping the almonds for the same quantity of mixed seeds. Don't be tempted to crank up the heat on your chargrill pan to cook these guys faster, or the sugar in the banana will make them catch and quickly char before cooking through.

SERVES 4 (MAKES 8)

Preparation time 5 minutes
Cooking time 6 minutes

2 tablespoons tapioca pearls
215 g (7½ oz/1⅓ cups) whole natural almonds
2 overripe bananas
4 eggs
macadamia oil, for cooking
Everyday spreadable butter (page 20), to serve
pure maple syrup, to serve

Mill the tapioca and almonds for **30 sec/speed 9**. Scrape down the side of the bowl. Add the bananas and eggs. Mix **for 20 sec/speed 4**.

Preheat a large chargrill pan over low heat and brush with the oil.

Pour 80 ml (2½ fl oz/⅓ cup) measures of the batter into rounds onto the pan. Cook, in batches, for 2 minutes on the first side, then 1 minute on the second side or until cooked and golden.

Serve the waffles warm with butter and maple syrup.

GLUTEN-FREE | PALEO | VEGETARIAN

BLUEBERRY BANANA LOAF

This is a sweet-tasting loaf but there are no added nasties — the sweetness comes from the overripe bananas and coconut. Wrap individual slices of this for adding to lunchboxes or freeze for up to 3 months. Once thawed, you can toast it before spreading with butter.

MAKES 1 LOAF (10 SLICES)

Preparation time 5 minutes
Cooking time 50 minutes + cooling

55 g (2 oz/1 cup) coconut flakes
75 g (2¾ oz/⅓ cup) whole wheat grains (see Note page 45)
145 g (5 oz/¾ cup) tapioca pearls
2 teaspoons baking powder
1 teaspoon ground cinnamon
2 overripe bananas, about 225 g (8 oz) in total, peeled and broken into 3
2 eggs
2 tablespoons pure maple syrup
125 g (4½ oz) frozen blueberries
Everyday spreadable butter (page 20), to serve

Preheat the oven to 180°C (350°F)/160°C (315°F) fan-forced. Line the base and sides of a 10 x 20 cm (4 x 8 inch) loaf (bar) tin with baking paper.

Mill the coconut, wheat grains and tapioca for **30 sec/speed 10**. Scrape down the side of the bowl.

Add the baking powder, cinnamon, bananas, eggs and maple syrup. Mix for **10 sec/speed 4**. Scrape down the side of the bowl. Add half the blueberries. Mix for **30 sec/reverse stir/speed 2**.

Spoon the mixture into the prepared tin and level the surface. Press the remaining blueberries over the surface of the loaf. Bake for 50 minutes or until cooked and golden. If you find that the top is browning too quickly, simply tent the pan with a piece of foil. Leave to cool in the tin for 15 minutes. Serve immediately with the everyday spreadable butter.

See photograph on pages 50–1.

NUT-FREE | VEGETARIAN

NOTE

I prefer to freeze my own berries. I simply place the berries into freezer-safe, resealable bags for easy stacking in the freezer.

SERVING SUGGESTION

You can serve this with Nut cream (page 15) instead of the Everyday spreadable butter.

BLUEBERRY BANANA LOAF
(PAGE 48)

SPICED PLUM SPREAD

This tastes like Christmas in a jar to me and is inspired by my local café, where they serve their own home-made seasonal jams with hot buttered toast. My dad was also a huge lover of plum jam. This version cuts out all the refined sugar.

MAKES 340 G (11¾ OZ/2½ CUPS)
Preparation time 5 minutes
Cooking time 10 minutes + cooling

1 kg (2 lb 4 oz) ripe plums, quartered and stones removed
½ teaspoon mixed (pumpkin pie) spice
2 teaspoons ground ginger
80 ml (2½ fl oz/⅓ cup) raw honey
1 tablespoon lemon juice
2 tablespoons chia seeds

Chop the plums for **3 sec/speed 6**. Scrape down the side of the bowl. Add the mixed spice, ginger, honey and lemon juice. Place the simmering basket, instead of the measuring cup, onto the mixer bowl lid. Cook for **10 min/90°C/speed 1**. Scrape down the side of the bowl. Leave to cool for 10 minutes in the bowl.

Add the chia seeds and mix for **2 min/speed 2**.

Transfer the plum mixture to sterilised jars (see Note). Leave to cool, then seal the jars. Use immediately or chill for up to 2 weeks.

DAIRY-FREE | GLUTEN-FREE | NUT-FREE | VEGETARIAN

NOTE
To sterilise jars, wash them in hot soapy water, rinse with hot water, then place (without any rubber seals) in a low (100°C/200°F, 80°C/175°F fan-forced) oven until completely dry.

STRAWBERRY SPREAD

Buy strawberries in abundance in summer when they are at their sweetest and cheapest price, then make some big batches of this spread and freeze it in 250 ml (9 fl oz/1 cup) measures for up to 6 months. I like to blend a few spoonfuls with milk and ice cubes for a yummy shake for the children.

MAKES 320 G (11¼ OZ/2 CUPS)

Preparation time 5 minutes
Cooking time 10 minutes + cooling

500 g (1 lb 2 oz) strawberries, hulled
2 teaspoons rosewater
2 tablespoons raw honey
1 tablespoon lemon juice
30 g (1 oz/¼ cup) chia seeds

Chop the strawberries for **2 sec/speed 5**. Scrape down the side of the bowl.

Add the rosewater and honey. Cook for **10 min/90°C/speed 1**. Scrape down the side of the bowl. Leave to cool for 10 minutes in the bowl.

Add the lemon and chia seeds and mix for **30 sec/reverse stir/speed 4**.

Transfer the strawberry mixture to sterilised jars (see Note on facing page). Cool, then seal the jars. Use immediately or chill for up to 2 weeks.

DAIRY-FREE | GLUTEN-FREE | NUT-FREE | PALEO | VEGETARIAN

KOREAN PANCAKES

These are so delicious crispy and hot straight from the frying pan and are a super fun breakfast to serve for the family. Tear them into sections, serve them with chopsticks, and allow kids to play away. These pancakes are also equally delicious eaten cold and popped into lunchboxes. You can also cook the batter in 2 tablespoon measures for a snack-sized option – any leftovers can be easily frozen (well wrapped) for up to 3 months. Simply thaw in the fridge and then either pan-fry again or reheat in the oven to crisp them up.

SERVES 4 (MAKES 4)

Preparation time 10 minutes
Cooking time 8 minutes

110 g (3¾ oz/½ cup) brown basmati rice
1 zucchini (courgette), cut into 3 crossways
1 small red capsicum (pepper), seeded and cut into 8 pieces
4 spring onions (scallions), cut into 5 cm (2 inch) lengths
2 eggs
125 ml (4 fl oz/½ cup) chilled water
60 g (2 oz/½ cup) bean sprouts
Garlic frying oil (page 21), for cooking

Mill the rice for **1 min/speed 10**. Scrape down the side of the bowl.

Add the zucchini, capsicum and spring onion. Chop for **30 sec/speed 4**. Scrape down the side of the bowl.

Add the eggs and the water. Mix for **30 sec/reverse stir/speed 3**. Scrape down the side of the bowl.

Add the bean sprouts. Mix for **30 sec/reverse stir/speed 1**.

Heat a little of the oil in a large frying pan over medium heat. Cook heaped ½ cup measures of the mixture, in batches, for 2 minutes each side or until cooked and golden. Serve warm.

DAIRY-FREE | GLUTEN-FREE | NUT-FREE | VEGETARIAN

SERVING SUGGESTIONS

For children, serve the pancakes with Tomato mix (page 28). For adults, serve with a spicy dipping sauce by combining 2 tablespoons tamari (gluten-free soy sauce), 1 tablespoon apple cider vinegar and 1 small seeded and thinly sliced red chilli.

MELT 'N' MIX BREAD

This is a great first baking recipe for the children to be involved with – it's too easy for words. Although tempting to eat warm, please have patience and allow the bread to cool in the pan completely before removing it to slice, as it's quite delicate when warm and may not hold its shape.

MAKES 1 LOAF (10 SLICES)

Preparation time 5 minutes
Cooking time 51 minutes + cooling

150 g (5½ oz) coconut flakes
125 g (4½ oz/¾ cup) linseeds (flaxseeds)
125 g (4½ oz) butter, chopped
1 teaspoon baking powder
2 teaspoons sea salt
4 eggs
1 tablespoon pure maple syrup
75 g (2¾ oz/½ cup) pepitas (pumpkin seeds)

Preheat the oven to 180°C (350°F)/160°C (315°F) fan-forced. Line the base and sides of a 10 x 20 cm (4 x 8 inch) loaf (bar) tin with baking paper.

Mill the coconut and linseeds for **30 sec/speed 10**. Transfer the milled mixture to a bowl.

Melt the butter for **1 min/100°C/speed 1**.

Return the milled mixture to the mixer bowl with the melted butter. Add the baking powder, salt, eggs and maple syrup. Mix for **20 sec/speed 5**.

Transfer the batter mixture to the prepared tin and level the surface. Press the pepitas on top. Bake for 50 minutes or until cooked and golden. Leave to cool in the pan. Serve sliced.

Chill any leftovers in an airtight container for up to 3 days and simply toast before serving.

GLUTEN-FREE | NUT-FREE | PALEO | VEGETARIAN

BAKED MAN-CAKE

Yep, it's a pancake – man-sized and deliciously filling with a dense, almost cake-like texture. If you are up for it, crisp some bacon slices in the frying pan first and then remove them before the batter goes in – the bacon makes a lovely salty topper with the maple syrup, and is a nod to my hubby's Canadian heritage.

SERVES 6

Preparation time 5 minutes
Cooking time 15 minutes

300 g (10½ oz/1⅓ cups) whole wheat grains (see Note page 45)
2 teaspoons baking powder
2 tablespoons pure maple syrup, plus extra to serve
2 eggs
375 ml (13 fl oz/1½ cups) milk of choice
1 teaspoon pure vanilla
2 tablespoons macadamia oil
Everyday spreadable butter (page 20), to serve

Preheat the oven to 200°C (400°F)/180°C (350°F) fan-forced. Preheat a 23 cm (9 inch) ovenproof frying pan over medium heat.

Mill the wheat grains for **1 min/speed 10**. Scrape down the side of the bowl. Add the baking powder, maple syrup, eggs, milk and the vanilla. Mix for **30 sec/speed 4**.

Add the oil to the hot frying pan and swirl to coat the base and side. Spoon in the batter, quickly tilting the pan so the mixture covers the base evenly. Immediately transfer the pan to the oven. Bake for 15 minutes or until cooked and golden.

Serve the pancake hot, straight from the pan, topped with butter and extra maple syrup.

VEGETARIAN

FAMILY FRITTER

All the lovely crispy texture and deliciousness of a fritter, but without having to stand over the stove flipping little rounds for what may seem like hours. There will be fights over who gets to eat the crispy corners, though, so be warned. Serve the fritter as is with fried, scrambled or poached eggs or see the topper suggestions below – the list is endless and you can tailor the flavour combos to suit every person's tastebuds in the house.

SERVES 4

Preparation time 10 minutes
Cooking time 40 minutes

55 g (2 oz/¼ cup) whole wheat grains (see Note page 45)
2 spring onions (scallions), cut into 5 cm (2 inch) lengths
1 handful flat-leaf (Italian) parsley leaves, plus extra to serve
400 g (14 oz) orange sweet potato, peeled and cut into
    3 cm (1¼ inch) pieces
4 zucchini (courgettes), cut into 3 pieces
2 eggs
1 teaspoon sea salt
¼ teaspoon ground white pepper
1 tablespoon Garlic frying oil (page 21)
basil leaves, to serve

Preheat the oven to 200°C (400°F)/180°C (350°F) fan-forced. Line a large baking tray with baking paper.

Mill the wheat grains for **1 min/speed 10**. Scrape down the side of the bowl. Add the spring onion and parsley. Chop for **5 sec/speed 5**. Scrape down the side of the bowl.

Add the sweet potato and zucchini. Chop for **3 sec/speed 5**. Scrape down the side of the bowl. Chop again for **3 sec/speed 5**. Scrape down the side of the bowl. Add the eggs, salt and pepper. Mix for **30 sec/speed 1**.

Spread the mixture evenly over the prepared tray, forming a 4 mm (³⁄₁₆ inch) thick rectangle. Bake for 40 minutes or until cooked, golden and crisp. Immediately brush the top with the oil. Serve immediately, topped with the basil and extra parsley or with your favourite toppers (see right).

DAIRY-FREE | NUT-FREE | VEGETARIAN

TOPPER OPTIONS AFTER BAKING

Fresh ricotta (page 12), Tomato mix (page 28), Super-greens pesto (page 25), Pear and pomegranate chutney (page 30), Fermented chopped salad (page 29), fresh herbs and lemon wedges.

THE BEST SCRAMBLED EGGS

It's a big call but I am happy to claim this title because, yes, these are decadent and, yes, they taste fantastic. There is nothing better than fluffy, creamy eggs for a heart-warming brekkie in my eyes. It just screams lazy weekends. Please don't skimp on the butter and cream — they're what separates this scramble from the standard.

SERVES 4

Preparation time 5 minutes
Cooking time 13 minutes

1 small handful mixed fresh herbs, such as tarragon, thyme, chives, flat-leaf (Italian) parsley, dill
50 g (1¾ oz) butter, chopped
125 ml (4 fl oz/½ cup) thin (pouring/whipping) cream
8 eggs

Chop the herbs for **5 sec/speed 5**. Scrape down the side of the bowl. Add the butter. Melt for **1 min/100°C/speed 1**. Scrape down the side of the bowl.

Insert the whisk attachment. Using a pastry brush, brush the whisk attachment and side of the mixer bowl with the melted butter mixture. Add the cream and the eggs. Whisk for **10 sec/speed 4**. Cook for **12 min/ 90°C/speed 2**. Serve hot.

GLUTEN-FREE | NUT-FREE | VEGETARIAN

BOILED EGG AND ASPARAGUS WITH SAGE BUTTER

Oh, my — crispy sage, asparagus and brown butter with boiled eggs is a match made in heaven. You can boost this little number into a brunch dish by adding some baby rocket (arugula) leaves and halved baby tomatoes.

SERVES 4
Preparation time 5 minutes
Cooking time 17 minutes

125 g (4½ oz) butter
4 tablespoons small sage leaves
1 teaspoon sea salt
4 eggs
2 bunches asparagus, trimmed
Melt 'n' mix bread (page 56), sliced, to serve

Cook the butter, sage and salt for **5 min/60°C/speed 2**. Transfer the butter mixture to a heatproof bowl.

Add 500 ml (17 fl oz/2 cups) water to the mixer bowl. Insert the simmering basket. Add the eggs.

Attach the steaming bowl, instead of the measuring cup, to the mixer bowl lid. Add the asparagus to the steaming bowl. Attach the steaming bowl lid and cook for **12 min/steam mode/speed 1**.

Transfer the asparagus to serving plates. Carefully remove the eggs, cool under running water, then peel them.

Add the eggs to the serving plates, break them open and spoon over the butter mixture. Serve immediately with the melt 'n' mix bread.

GLUTEN-FREE | PALEO | VEGETARIAN

MY IRISH POTATO RÖSTI

My dad was Irish, which meant we ate a deliciously large volume of potatoes at every meal when I was growing up. On Friday nights my mum would cook a 'fry-up' for dinner, which included eggs, bacon, beans, sausage, pan-fried buttery potato bread and toasted soda bread – all served with lashings of HP Sauce. My version of potato bread is more like potato rösti, with its delicate texture, and includes fresh thyme. It's cooked in a garlic-flavoured oil for a savoury brekkie side. Or, you can fry it up in macadamia oil if you'd prefer to spread it with Spiced plum spread (page 52) or honey instead. The children will enjoy dipping it into Tomato mix (page 28).

MAKES 8

Preparation time 10 minutes
Cooking time 33 minutes + cooling

75 g (2¾ oz/¼ cup) whole wheat grains (see Note page 45)
500 g (1 lb 2 oz) floury potatoes, peeled, cut into
    2 cm (¾ inch) pieces
2 teaspoons sea salt
125 ml (4 fl oz/½ cup) milk of choice
80 g (2¾ oz) butter, chopped
2 egg yolks
2 teaspoons thyme leaves
¼ teaspoon ground white pepper
Garlic frying oil (page 21), for cooking

Mill the wheat grains for **1 min/speed 10**. Transfer the milled wheat to a bowl.

Insert the whisk attachment into the mixer bowl. Add the potato, salt and milk. Attach the simmering basket, instead of the measuring cup, to the mixer bowl lid. Cook for **25 min/95°C/speed 1**.

Add the butter, yolks, thyme and pepper. Mix for **20 sec/speed 3**. Scrape down the side of the bowl. Add the milled wheat. Mix for **20 sec/speed 3**. Transfer to a heatproof bowl. Cool to room temperature then chill for 1 hour or until firm.

Heat a large frying pan over medium–high heat and liberally brush with the oil. Place 80 ml (2½ fl oz/⅓ cup) measures of the potato mixture into the pan, flattening to a 3 mm (⅛ inch) thickness. Cook, in batches, for 2 minutes each side or until golden. Serve immediately.

VEGETARIAN

NOTE

You can also cook these a little thicker in a pattie-style, if desired. However, be sure to use fresh floury potatoes so the patties hold their shape when cooked.

BEANS AND GREENS

These are just the easiest, tastiest beans around. These are a huge hit in our house, and you just know that everyone will have happy, full bellies right through until lunchtime. Try using chickpeas or black beans instead and you can swap the coriander for flat-leaf (Italian) parsley, too.

SERVES 4

Preparation time 5 minutes
Cooking time 10 minutes

1 brown onion, peeled and quartered
1 long red chilli, halved and seeded
1 tablespoon rosemary leaves
2 tomatoes, cored and quartered
4 large kale leaves, white stalks removed, torn into
    5 cm (2 inch) pieces
2 teaspoons smoked paprika
1 tablespoon Stock 'cube' of choice (pages 34–5)
2 tablespoons Tomato mix (page 28)
340 g (12 oz/2 cups) cooked red kidney beans (see page 37)
125 ml (4 fl oz/½ cup) water
1 handful coriander (cilantro) leaves

Chop the onion, chilli and rosemary for **5 sec/speed 7**. Scrape down the side of the bowl.

Add the tomato and kale. Chop for **3 sec/speed 5**. Scrape down the side of the bowl.

Add all the remaining ingredients. Cook for **10 min/120°C/reverse stir/ speed 2**. Serve immediately.

DAIRY-FREE | GLUTEN-FREE | NUT-FREE | VEGAN | VEGETARIAN

AVOCADO PÂTÉ

When avocados are cheap, this is what fills our fridge. Jam-packed full of healthy fats, this avo pâté is just delicious spread over your favourite toasted bread in the morning. It's also great served as a snack with a few seeded crackers and vegetable sticks.

SERVES 4

Preparation time 10 minutes

1 handful flat-leaf (Italian) parsley leaves
2 avocados, peeled, seeded and quartered
finely grated zest and juice of 1 small lemon
115 g (4 oz/½ cup) Fresh ricotta (page 12)
1 teaspoon sea salt
¼ teaspoon ground white pepper
1 tablespoon avocado oil

Chop the parsley and avocado for **3 sec/speed 7**. Scrape down the bowl.

Add all the remaining ingredients. Mix for **5 sec/speed 7**.

Serve immediately in individual ramekins or cover the surface tightly to prevent browning and chill the pâté for up to 2 days.

GLUTEN-FREE | NUT-FREE | VEGETARIAN

NOTE

Make this vegan and paleo-friendly by swapping the ricotta for Nut cream (page 15). Add an extra dash of avocado oil or water when blending.

CORNBREAD BISCUITS

I was introduced to savoury 'biscuits' on my first visit to Canada when visiting family. They are quite close to a scone, but just flatter. You can serve them as a side to soup or a starter. Being slightly sweet and slightly savoury means you can either top them with just butter or your favourite sweet spread.

MAKES 14

Preparation time 10 minutes
Cooking time 20 minutes

220 g (7¾ oz/1 cup) popping corn kernels
115 g (4 oz/½ cup) whole wheat grains (see Note page 45)
2 teaspoons baking powder
40 g (1½ oz) butter, at room temperature
125 ml (4 fl oz/½ cup) milk of choice
1 tablespoon lemon juice
1 egg
1 tablespoon raw honey
1 corn cob, kernels removed

Preheat the oven to 180°C (350°F)/160°C (315°F) fan-forced. Line two large baking trays with baking paper.

Mill the popping corn kernels and wheat grains for **1 min/speed 10**. Scrape down the side of the bowl.

Add the baking powder, butter, milk, lemon juice, egg and honey. Mix for **10 sec/speed 4**. Scrape down the side of the bowl. Add the fresh corn kernels. Mix for **5 sec/speed 7**.

Spoon 2 tablespoon measures of the mixture into rounds onto the prepared trays, leaving 4 cm (1½ inch) space between each one to allow for spreading. Bake both trays on separate oven racks for 20 minutes, swapping the trays halfway through cooking, or until the biscuits are cooked and golden. Serve immediately.

VEGETARIAN

SERVING SUGGESTIONS

Fresh ricotta (page 12), Spiced plum spread (page 52) or Pear and pomegranate chutney (page 30).

SPINACH AND CORN TORTILLAS

This is double yum, and once you make it from scratch at home, you will never go back to purchasing a store-bought variety of tortilla. Fill these guys with scrambled eggs or chopped tomato or use them to wrap around your favourite fillings for lunch.

MAKES 8

Preparation time 5 minutes
Cooking time 20 minutes

115 g (4 oz/½ cup) popping corn kernels
50 g (1¾ oz) baby English spinach leaves
6 eggs
60 ml (2 fl oz/¼ cup) milk of choice
Garlic frying oil (page 21), for cooking

Mill the corn for **1 min/speed 9**. Scrape down the side of the bowl. Add the spinach. Chop for **30 sec/speed 7**. Scrape down the side of the bowl. Add the eggs and the milk. Mix for **1 min/speed 4**.

Heat a large frying pan over medium heat and brush liberally with the oil. Pour a ¼ cup measure of the mixture into the pan, quickly tilting to cover the base to form a 14 cm (5½ inch) round. Cook for 2 minutes or until cooked through. Turn over and cook for another 30 seconds.

Transfer the tortillas to a plate and cover to keep warm. Repeat with the remaining spinach mixture. Serve immediately, or eat them cold.

GLUTEN-FREE | NUT-FREE | VEGETARIAN

NOTES

If making ahead, cook and layer the tortillas between sheets of baking paper to make them easier to separate before serving.

Be sure to use a good amount of oil when cooking, otherwise these tortillas can catch easily on the base of the pan.

MUESLI BISCUITS

These biscuits are great with a cup of tea if you are still quite full from a big dinner the night before. They also transport well, so are wonderful to take to a loved one (especially the ones you know are brekkie skippers) or to pack in lunchboxes. Totally moreish while still warm straight from the oven, it's hard to stop at just one.

MAKES 26

Preparation time 10 minutes
Cooking time 25 minutes + cooling

1 green apple, quartered and cored
100 g (3½ oz/1 cup) rolled (porridge) oats
230 g (8½ oz/1½ cups) mixed seeds, such as pepitas
    (pumpkin seeds), sunflower seeds, sesame seeds
60 ml (2 fl oz/¼ cup) pure maple syrup
1 teaspoon ground ginger
1 egg

Preheat the oven to 180°C (350°F)/160°C (315°F) fan-forced. Line two large baking trays with baking paper.

Chop the apple for **3 sec/speed 5**. Scrape down the side of the bowl. Add the oats, seeds, maple syrup and ginger. Mix for **20 sec/speed 5**. Scrape down the side of the bowl. Add the egg. Mix for **5 sec/reverse stir/speed 5**.

Spoon tablespoon measures of the mixture into rounds on the prepared trays, pressing to flatten into 4 cm (1½ inch) rounds.

Bake both trays on separate oven racks for 25 minutes, swapping the trays halfway during cooking, or until the biscuits are golden. Leave them to cool on the trays for 10 minutes then serve.

DAIRY-FREE | NUT-FREE | VEGETARIAN

STRAWBERRY AND COCONUT CHIA PUDDING

This is a particular favourite of mine — I love the ease of preparation and tummy-filling qualities these chia puddings have. The mixture will keep chilled for up to 3 days so make a double quantity and then you know breakfast is sorted for at least a couple of days. Substitute any seasonal fresh fruit you have on-hand.

SERVES 4

Preparation time 5 minutes
Standing time 10 minutes + chilling

110 g (3¾ oz/2 cups) coconut flakes
2 tablespoons pure maple syrup, plus 1 teaspoon extra
130 g (4½ oz/⅔ cup) chia seeds
250 g (9 oz) strawberries, hulled
2 teaspoons rosewater

Mill the coconut for **30 sec/speed 9**. Scrape down the side of the bowl.

Add 330 ml (11¼ fl oz/1⅓ cups) water, the maple syrup and chia seeds. Mix for **30 sec/speed 4**.

Transfer to a jug and leave to stand for 10 minutes, stirring occasionally, or until the chia seeds are plump and the mixture firms slightly.

Reserve 4 strawberries for serving. Blend the remaining strawberries, rosewater and extra maple syrup for **10 sec/speed 5**. Scrape down the side of the bowl. Blend again for **20 sec/speed 9**.

Spoon half the strawberry mixture into four serving glasses. Spoon over the chia mixture, then top with the remaining strawberry mixture and reserved strawberries. Chill for at least 1 hour then serve.

DAIRY-FREE | GLUTEN-FREE | NUT-FREE | PALEO | VEGAN | VEGETARIAN

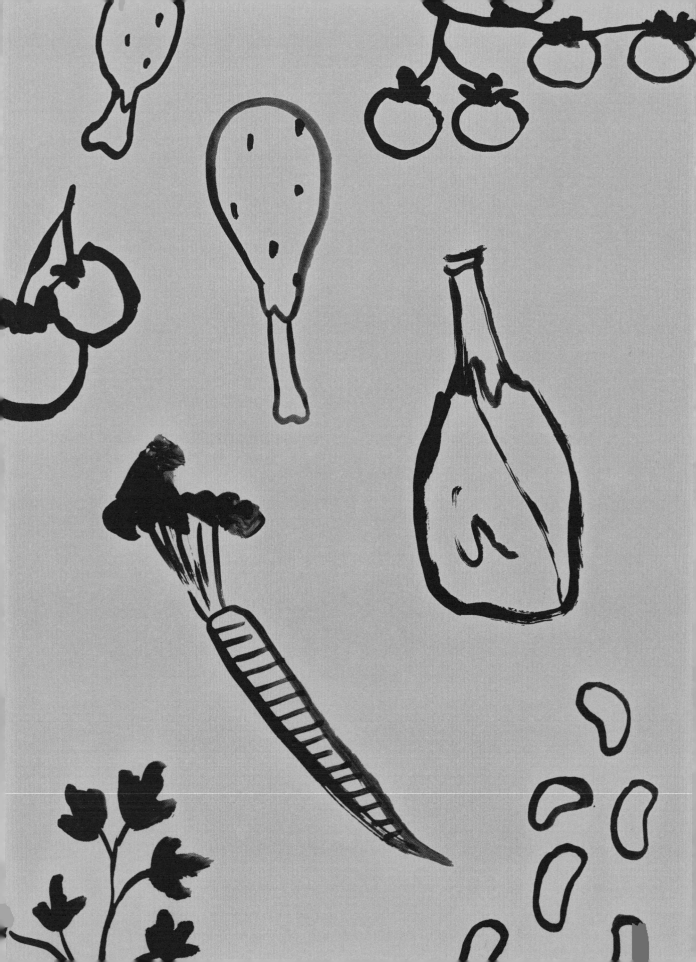

soulful
soups

BENEFICIAL BROTHS

GOLDEN CHICKEN BROTH

A cup of this tasty broth is wonderful for a mid-morning or afternoon snack – not to mention a beautiful stock to add to any of your favourite soup recipes. If you plan to freeze the stock, be sure to do so in 250 ml (9 fl oz/1 cup) measures. That way you can simply thaw as small or large a quantity as you need.

MAKES 1.25 LITRES (44 FL OZ/5 CUPS)

Preparation time 10 minutes
Cooking time 30 minutes + cooling

1 red onion, peeled and quartered
2 carrots, cut into 3
1 baby fennel bulb, trimmed and quartered
2 garlic cloves
3 cm (1¼ inch) piece fresh turmeric
1 tablespoon apple cider vinegar
500 g (1 lb 2 oz) organic chicken wings
sea salt, to taste

Chop the onion, carrot, fennel, garlic and turmeric for **5 sec/speed 5**. Scrape down the side of the bowl.

Add the vinegar and chicken wings, then fill the mixer with enough water to reach the capacity line on the inside of your mixer bowl. Cook for **30 min/90°C/reverse stir/speed 1**.

Set a large sieve over a large bowl. Strain the mixture through the sieve, discarding the solids. Taste and then season with salt. Use immediately or leave to cool then chill in airtight containers for up to 1 week, or freeze for up to 6 months.

DAIRY-FREE | GLUTEN-FREE | NUT-FREE | PALEO

ROASTED
BEEF BONE
BROTH
(PAGE 76)

GOLDEN
CHICKEN
BROTH
(FACING
PAGE)

ROASTED BEEF BONE BROTH

Roasting the ingredients before making this broth gives a delicious meaty flavour and adds a little sweetness due to the caramelising of the meat and fat. Try to get osso bucco pieces that have a really large centre marrow bone. This will add even more beneficial gelatine to your bone broth, giving you amazing gut-healing benefits.

MAKES 1.1 LITRES (38 FL OZ)
Preparation time 10 minutes
Cooking time 1 hour + cooling

1 brown onion, peeled and quartered
2 carrots, cut into 3
2 celery stalks, cut into 5 cm (2 inch) lengths
1 kg (2 lb 4 oz) small beef osso bucco
2 garlic cloves
1 rosemary sprig
1 tablespoon apple cider vinegar
sea salt, to taste

Preheat the oven to 220°C (425°F)/200°C (400°F) fan-forced. Line a large baking tray with baking paper.

Chop the onion, carrot and celery for **5 sec/speed 5**.

Transfer the mixture to the prepared tray and top with the osso bucco meat and bones. Bake for 30 minutes, turning the beef once, until golden and caramelised.

Transfer the mixture to the mixer bowl, making sure you scrape all the flavourings from the paper on the baking tray.

Add the garlic, rosemary and vinegar, then fill the mixer with enough water to reach the capacity line on the inside of your mixer bowl. Cook for **30 min/90°C/soft stir**.

Set a large sieve over a large bowl and line it with muslin (cheesecloth). Strain the mixture through the muslin, discarding the solids. Taste and then season with salt. Use the broth immediately, or allow to cool then chill in airtight containers for up to 1 week, or freeze for up to 6 months.

DAIRY-FREE | GLUTEN-FREE | NUT-FREE | PALEO

SMOOTH AND CREAMY

CARROT AND SWEDE SOUP

The favourite side dish that my mum made while I was growing up was carrot and swede mash – the creamy combination of the two vegetables, with the added bonus of the sweetness from the carrots, is just heavenly. I now whip it into a soup version, which my family always devour without any complaint. The fennel seeds give it an extra lift.

SERVES 4

Preparation time 5 minutes
Cooking time 25 minutes

1 brown onion, peeled and quartered
2 celery stalks, cut into 4 cm (1½ inch) lengths
6 carrots, cut into 3
1 swede, peeled and cut into 2 cm (¾ inch) pieces
1 tablespoon Garlic frying oil (page 21)
2 teaspoons fennel seeds
1 tablespoon Stock 'cube' of choice (pages 34–5)
125 ml (4 fl oz/½ cup) Coconut milk (page 17)

Chop the onion, celery, carrot and swede for **5 sec/speed 5**. Scrape down the side of the bowl. Add the oil and cook for **5 min/100°C/speed 1**. Scrape down the side of the bowl.

Add the fennel seeds, stock cube and 750 ml (26 fl oz/3 cups water). Cook for **20 min/100°C/speed 1**.

Blend for **1 min/speed 5**, slowly increasing to **speed 8**. Add the coconut milk and mix for **10 sec/speed 2**. Serve immediately or chill in an airtight container for up to 3 days or freeze for up to 3 months.

DAIRY-FREE | GLUTEN-FREE | NUT-FREE | PALEO | VEGAN | VEGETARIAN

SERVING SUGGESTIONS

Cauliflower focaccia (page 164), Cornbread biscuits (page 66).

GINGER SWEET POTATO SOUP

Sweet-tasting and super creamy, this soup really hits the spot. I always add a sprinkling of dried chilli flakes to my serve for added spice.

SERVES 4
Preparation time 5 minutes
Cooking time 25 minutes

1 red onion, peeled and quartered
2 garlic cloves
3 cm (1¼ inch) piece fresh ginger, peeled
600 g (1 lb 5 oz) orange sweet potato, peeled and
    cut into 3 cm (1¼ inch) pieces
2 carrots, cut into 3
1 tablespoon Stock 'cube' of choice (pages 34–5)
50 g (1¾ oz) butter, chopped

Chop the onion, garlic and ginger for **5 sec/speed 7**. Scrape down the side of the bowl.

Add the sweet potato, carrot, stock cube and 500 ml (17 fl oz/2 cups) water. Cook for **25 min/100°C/speed 1**.

Add the butter and blend for **1 min/speed 5**, slowly increasing to speed 8. Season with freshly ground black pepper and serve immediately or chill in an airtight container for up to 3 days.

GLUTEN-FREE | NUT-FREE | VEGETARIAN |

SERVING
SUGGESTIONS

Toasted slices of Melt 'n' mix bread (page 56), My Irish potato rösti (page 62).

MEXICAN TOMATO SOUP

This soup is deceptively hearty, but you can beef it up even more by adding some cooked red kidney beans (see page 37). This is a great soup as you can either tone down or turn up the spices to suit, and it's easy to freeze.

SERVES 4
Preparation time 5 minutes
Cooking time 30 minutes

1 red onion, peeled and quartered
1 red capsicum (pepper), seeded and cut into 8
1 tablespoon Garlic frying oil (page 21)
2 teaspoons ground cumin
1 teaspoon sweet paprika
1 pinch ground chilli
500 g (1 lb 2 oz) tomatoes, cored and quartered
1 tablespoon Stock 'cube' of choice (pages 34–5)
1 small handful coriander (cilantro) leaves
avocado oil, to serve

Chop the onion and capsicum for **5 sec/speed 5**. Scrape down the side of the bowl.

Add the oil, cumin, paprika and chilli. Cook for **5 min/100°C/speed 1**. Scrape down the side of the bowl.

Add the tomato and chop for **3 sec/speed 5**. Scrape down the side of the bowl. Add the stock cube and 500 ml (17 fl oz/2 cups) water. Cook for **25 min/100°C/speed 1**.

Blend for **1 min/speed 5**, slowly increasing to **speed 8**. Serve hot, topped with the coriander and drizzled with the avocado oil. Season with freshly ground black pepper. Chill in an airtight container for up to 3 days or freeze for up to 3 months.

DAIRY-FREE | GLUTEN-FREE | NUT-FREE | PALEO | VEGAN | VEGETARIAN

SERVING SUGGESTIONS
Spinach and corn tortillas (page 68), Cornbread biscuits (page 66).

CREAMED GREENS SOUP

This is a soup that is equally delicious served hot in winter or chilled in the warmer months. You will be amazed at how refreshing it can be, especially if you add a handful of fresh mint leaves.

SERVES 4
Preparation time 5 minutes
Cooking time 20 minutes

4 spring onions (scallions), cut into 4 cm (1½ inch) lengths
2 garlic cloves
2 celery stalks, cut into 4 cm (1½ inch) lengths
2 zucchini (courgettes), cut into 3
50 g (1¾ oz) butter
140 g (5 oz/1 cup) frozen peas
1 tablespoon Stock 'cube' of choice (pages 34–5)
1 large handful basil leaves
80 ml (2½ fl oz/⅓ cup) Cow's milk yoghurt (page 14)

Chop the spring onion, garlic, celery and zucchini for **5 sec/speed 5**. Scrape down the side of the bowl. Add the butter and cook for **5 min/100°C/speed 1**. Scrape down the side of the bowl.

Add the peas, stock cube and 750 ml (26 fl oz/3 cups) water. Cook for **15 min/100°C/speed 1**.

Add the basil and blend for **1 min/speed 5**, slowly increasing to **speed 8**.

Add the yoghurt and mix for **20 sec/speed 2**. Serve immediately. Chill in an airtight container for up to 3 days or freeze for up to 3 months.

GLUTEN-FREE | NUT-FREE | VEGETARIAN

SERVING SUGGESTIONS

Cauliflower focaccia (page 164), Cornbread biscuits (page 66).

HEARTY

POTATO AND CORN CHOWDER

Although not technically a 'real' chowder, this is pretty darn close in terms of taste and creaminess. If you like, you can fold through some freshly cooked prawns (shrimp) or flaked, smoked trout.

SERVES 4

Preparation time 10 minutes
Cooking time 20 minutes

1 brown onion, peeled and quartered
2 celery stalks, cut into 4 cm (1½ inch) lengths
1 garlic clove
50 g (1¾ oz) butter, chopped
750 ml (26 fl oz/3 cups) full-cream (whole) cow's milk
2 floury potatoes, total weight 400 g (14 oz), peeled and
    cut into 2 cm (¾ inch) pieces
2 corn cobs, kernels removed
1 tablespoon Stock 'cube' of choice (pages 34–5)
2 teaspoons lemon thyme leaves

Chop the onion, celery and garlic for **5 sec/speed 5**. Scrape down the side of the bowl.

Add the butter and cook for **5 min/100°C/speed 1**. Scrape down the side of the bowl.

Add the milk, potato, corn, stock cube, 125 ml (4 fl oz/½ cup) water and the lemon thyme. Cook for **15 min/90°C/speed 1**. Serve hot. Left-over chowder can be chilled in an airtight container for up to 3 days.

GLUTEN-FREE | NUT-FREE | VEGETARIAN

SERVING SUGGESTION

Cornbread biscuits (page 66).

VEGETABLE LAKSA WITH RICE

I always feel that laksa is such an indulgent soup – the robust flavour combinations and super creamy taste from the coconut milk do more than make my heart sing. If you like, add some cooked chicken or prawns (shrimp) to your serving bowls first. However, I think you will find the abundance of vegetables and rice in this soup is more than hearty enough for even the biggest of appetites.

SERVES 4

Preparation time 15 minutes
Cooking time 10 minutes

2 tablespoons Asian paste (page 32)
2 teaspoons ground turmeric
500 ml (17 fl oz/2 cups) Coconut milk (page 17)
100 g (3½ oz/½ cup) brown basmati rice, rinsed
1 carrot, halved lengthways and sliced diagonally
125 g (4½ oz) baby corn, halved lengthways
1 bunch baby bok choy (pak choy), quartered lengthways
1 red capsicum (pepper), seeded and cut into
    3 cm (1¼ inch) pieces
115 g (4 oz/1 cup) bean sprouts
1 handful Thai basil leaves

Add the Asian paste, turmeric, coconut milk and 500 ml (17 fl oz/2 cups) water to the mixer bowl. Add the rinsed rice to the simmering basket, then insert it into the mixer bowl.

Attach the steaming bowl, instead of the measuring cup, to the mixer bowl lid.

Add the ingredients to the steaming bowl in the following order: carrot, baby corn, bok choy and capsicum. Attach the steaming bowl lid. Cook for **10 min/steam mode/speed 1**.

Divide the vegetables among four serving bowls. Spoon in the rice, then pour over the coconut milk mixture. Top with the bean sprouts and basil leaves. Serve hot or chill in an airtight container for up to 3 days.

DAIRY-FREE | GLUTEN-FREE | NUT-FREE | VEGAN | VEGETARIAN

ASIAN PORK MEATBALL SOUP

There is so much flavour packed into this soup, and the meatballs are so tasty and moist, that it will definitely be gobbled up super fast.

SERVES 4
Preparation time 15 minutes
Cooking time 20 minutes

2 spring onions (scallions), cut into 4 cm (1½ inch) lengths
1 garlic clove
2 tablespoons Asian paste (page 32), plus 1 extra tablespoon
500 g (1 lb 2 oz) minced (ground) pork
1 bunch snake (yard-long) beans, trimmed and cut into
    5 cm (2 inch) lengths (see Note)
4 Chinese cabbage (wong bok) leaves, thinly shredded
tamari (gluten-free soy sauce), to serve
sliced red chilli, to serve

Chop the spring onion, garlic and Asian paste for **5 sec/speed 5**. Scrape down the side of the bowl. Add the minced pork and mix for **20 sec/speed 5**.

Shape 1 tablespoon measures of the mixture into meatballs (makes 20).

Add the extra Asian paste and 1 litre (35 fl oz/4 cups) water to the mixer bowl. Insert the simmering basket. Add the meatballs to the simmering basket and attach the lid.

Attach the steaming bowl, instead of the measuring cup, to the mixer bowl lid. Add the beans, then the cabbage. Attach the steaming bowl lid and cook for **20 min/steam mode/speed 2**.

Transfer the steamed vegetables to serving bowls. Separate and add the meatballs and pour over the soup mixture. Serve hot with the tamari and chilli. Chill in an airtight container for up to 3 days or freeze for up to 3 months.

DAIRY-FREE | GLUTEN-FREE | NUT-FREE

NOTE
If you are unable to purchase snake beans, you can simply substitute 200 g (7 oz) trimmed green beans.

SPICY THAI CHICKEN SOUP

The sensory blast of this soup makes it the perfect pick-me-up if you are feeling under the weather. It's sure to have you breathing clearly in no time.

SERVES 4

Preparation time 10 minutes
Cooking time 15 minutes + standing

2 tablespoons Asian paste (page 32)
2 teaspoons Tomato mix (page 28)
2 skinless chicken breast fillets, cut into 2 cm (¾ inch) pieces
4 kaffir lime leaves, torn
1 lemongrass stem, pale part only, cut into
    3 cm (1¼ inch) lengths, bruised
2 long red chillies, thinly sliced
250 g (9 oz) cherry tomatoes, halved
200 g (7 oz) button mushrooms, halved
2 teaspoons honey
1 teaspoon tamari (gluten-free soy sauce)
1 tablespoon lime juice
coriander (cilantro) leaves, to serve

Cook the Asian paste, tomato mix, 1 litre (35 fl oz/4 cups) water, the chicken, lime leaves, lemongrass and chilli for **15 min/100°C/reverse stir/speed 2**.

Add the tomato, mushroom, honey, tamari and lime juice. Mix for **10 sec/reverse stir/speed 2**. Leave to stand, covered, for 5 minutes. Remove and discard the lime leaf and lemongrass. Serve hot, topped with the coriander. Chill in an airtight container for up to 3 days.

DAIRY-FREE | GLUTEN-FREE | NUT-FREE | PALEO

HARIRA SOUP

The spice combination in this delicious Moroccan-style soup is tremendously warming. I have never come across anyone who hasn't fallen in love with a bowl of this fragrant soup.

SERVES 4

Preparation time 10 minutes
Cooking time 25 minutes

1 red onion, peeled and quartered
2 celery stalks, cut into 4 cm (1½ inch) lengths
2 carrots, cut into 3
2 garlic cloves
2 cm (¾ inch) piece fresh ginger, peeled
50 g (1¾ oz) butter, chopped
2 teaspoons cumin seeds
1 pinch saffron threads
500 g (1 lb 2 oz) tomatoes, cored and quartered
1 tablespoon Tomato mix (page 28)
200 g (7 oz/1 cup) cooked chickpeas (see page 37)
750 ml (26 fl oz/3 cups) Golden chicken broth (page 74)
50 g (1¾ oz/¼ cup) split red lentils
1 cinnamon stick
small mint leaves, to serve
lemon wedges, to serve

Chop the onion, celery, carrot, garlic and ginger for **3 sec/speed 5**. Scrape down the side of the bowl.

Add the butter, cumin and saffron. Cook for **5 min/100°C/reverse stir/ speed 1**. Scrape down the side of the bowl.

Add the tomato and chop for **2 sec/speed 5**. Scrape down the side of the bowl.

Add the tomato mix, chickpeas, broth, lentils and cinnamon stick. Cook for **20 min/100°C/speed 1**. Remove and discard the cinnamon stick and serve the soup hot, topped with the mint leaves and the lemon wedges served on the side. Chill in an airtight container for up to 3 days or freeze for up to 3 months.

See photograph on pages 90–1.

GLUTEN-FREE | NUT-FREE

VARIATION

For a vegetarian or vegan meal, simply swap the Golden chicken broth for a vegetable stock.

HARIRA SOUP (PAGE 88)

PRAWN GUMBO-ISH SOUP

This is a bit of a twist on a southern United States staple, but all the hearty flavours are present.

SERVES 4

Preparation time 10 minutes
Cooking time 27 minutes

1 brown onion, peeled and quartered
2 spring onions (scallions), cut into 4 cm (1½ inch) lengths
2 red capsicums (peppers), seeded and cut into 8
2 garlic cloves
2 teaspoons dried thyme
1 teaspoon dried marjoram
50 g (1¾ oz) butter, chopped
500 g (1 lb 2 oz) tomatoes, cored and quartered
1 tablespoon Stock 'cube' of choice (pages 34–5)
2 fresh bay leaves
600 g (1 lb 5 oz) peeled, deveined raw king prawns
   (jumbo shrimp)
1 tablespoon lemon juice
flat-leaf (Italian) parsley leaves, to serve

Chop the onion, spring onion, capsicum and garlic for **5 sec/speed 5**. Scrape down the side of the bowl.

Add the thyme, marjoram and butter and cook for **15 min/100°C/ speed 1**. Scrape down the side of the bowl. Add the tomato and chop for **10 sec/speed 5**.

Add the stock cube, bay leaves, 250 ml (9 fl oz/1 cup) water, the prawns and lemon juice. Cook for **12 min/100°C/reverse stir/speed 2**. Serve hot, topped with the parsley. Chill in an airtight container for up to 3 days or freeze for up to 3 months.

GLUTEN-FREE | NUT-FREE | PALEO

SERVING SUGGESTIONS

Spread some Smoky avo mayo (see page 26) over Melt 'n' mix bread (page 56) or Cauliflower focaccia (page 164).

BEEF AND BARLEY SOUP

This is a quicker version of a classic with all the same flavours. Browning the meat separately in a frying pan gives an added boost of beefiness.

SERVES 4

Preparation time 5 minutes
Cooking time 1 hour

300 g (10½ oz) minced (ground) beef
50 g (1¾ oz) butter
1 brown onion, peeled and quartered
2 carrots, cut into 3
2 celery stalks, cut into 4 cm (1½ inch) lengths
1 tablespoon Stock 'cube' of choice (pages 34–5)
1 litre (35 fl oz/4 cups) Roasted beef bone broth (page 76)
1 rosemary sprig
2 fresh bay leaves
100 g (3½ oz/½ cup) pearl barley

Heat a large frying pan over high heat. Add the minced beef and cook, stirring, to break up any lumps, for 5 minutes. Add the butter and cook, stirring, for 5 minutes or until the butter melts and the beef is golden brown. Set aside.

Chop the onion, carrot and celery for **3 sec/speed 5**. Scrape down the side of the bowl.

Add the browned beef mixture to the bowl (making sure you scrape up all flavourings from the base of the pan), the stock cube, broth, rosemary, bay leaves and barley. Cook for **50 min/100°C/speed 1**. Remove and discard the rosemary and bay leaves. Serve hot. Chill in an airtight container for up to 3 days or freeze for up to 3 months.

NUT-FREE

MUMMY'S CHICKEN SOUP

Soup for the soul – a bowl of this cures all the world's problems and then some. The abundance of fresh flat-leaf parsley and the use of the Golden chicken broth are what make this truly satisfying.

SERVES 4

Preparation time 10 minutes
Cooking time 30 minutes

1 bunch flat-leaf (Italian) parsley, cut in half
1 leek, white part only, cut into 4 cm (1½ inch) lengths
2 carrots, cut into 3
2 baby fennel bulbs, trimmed and cut into 3 cm (1¼ inch) pieces
1 tablespoon Garlic frying oil (page 21)
2 large skinless chicken thigh fillets, cut into 1 cm (½ inch) pieces
1 teaspoon fennel seeds
1 tablespoon Stock 'cube' of choice (pages 34–5)
1 litre (35 fl oz/4 cups) Golden chicken broth (page 74)
1 zucchini (courgette), finely chopped

Chop the parsley for **5 sec/speed 5**. Transfer to a bowl and set aside.

Chop the leek, carrot and fennel bulb for **5 sec/speed 5**. Scrape down the side of the bowl. Add the oil and cook for **10 min/100°C/speed 1**.

Add the chicken, fennel seeds, stock cube and broth. Cook for **20 min/100°C/reverse stir/speed 2**.

Add the zucchini and reserved parsley. Mix for **20 sec/reverse stir/ speed 2**. Leave to stand, covered, for 3 minutes then serve hot. Chill in an airtight container for up to 3 days or freeze for up to 3 months.

DAIRY-FREE | GLUTEN-FREE | NUT-FREE | PALEO

delicious
mains

CHICKEN AND PORK

PORK PATTIES

This is a great and versatile mid-week meal. Serve with mashed potato and Simple buttery veg (page 166) or as a burger (see suggestions below).

SERVES 4

Preparation time 10 minutes
Cooking time 10 minutes

3 teaspoons fennel seeds
½ teaspoon black peppercorns
1 teaspoon sea salt
1 baby fennel bulb, trimmed and cut into 3
2 spring onions (scallions), trimmed and cut into
    5 cm (2 inch) lengths
1 large handful flat-leaf (Italian) parsley leaves
500 g (1 lb 2 oz) minced (ground) pork
2 tablespoons Garlic frying oil (page 21)
lime wedges, to serve
micro herbs, such as rocket (arugula) or sorrel, to garnish

SERVING SUGGESTIONS

Serve sandwiched between your favourite burger buns, dollop with Avo mayo (page 26), Fermented chopped salad (page 29), Quick pickled vegies (page 150), Broccoli and cashew tabouleh (page 154) and your favourite salad ingredients.

NOTE

You can purchase micro herbs from large supermarkets and greengrocers. If unavailable, simply use some chopped flat-leaf (Italian) parsley instead.

Mill the fennel seeds, peppercorns and sea salt for **30 sec/speed 9**. Scrape down the side of the bowl.

Add the fennel bulb, spring onion and parsley. Chop for **5 sec/speed 7**. Scrape down the side of the bowl.

Add the minced pork and mix for **1 min/speed 4**.

With slightly damp hands, shape the mixture into four patties.

Heat the oil in a large frying pan over medium–high heat. Cook the patties for 10 minutes, turning once, or until golden and cooked. Serve with the lime wedges and garnish with the micro herbs.

DAIRY-FREE | GLUTEN-FREE | NUT-FREE | PALEO

CREAMY PESTO CHICKEN

Traditionally this is a dish that's served with wheat pasta, but here I have given it a vegie boost instead. You could also serve it spooned over cooked brown rice, mashed potato or with a big bowl of crisp garden greens.

SERVES 4

Preparation time 10 minutes
Cooking time 12 minutes

500 ml (17 fl oz/2 cups) Coconut milk (page 17)
1 red onion, cut into thin wedges
2 large skinless chicken breast fillets, halved lengthways, thinly sliced crossways
250 g (9 oz) red cabbage, thinly sliced
6 zucchini (courgettes), peeled into thin lengths with a vegetable peeler
80 g (2¾ oz/⅓ cup) Super-greens pesto (page 25)

Add the coconut milk, onion and chicken to the mixer bowl and attach the lid.

Attach the steaming bowl, instead of the measuring cup, to the mixer bowl lid. Add the cabbage, then the zucchini, to the steaming bowl. Attach the steaming bowl lid. Cook for **12 min/steam mode/reverse stir/speed 1**. Transfer the vegetables to serving plates.

Add the pesto to the chicken mixture. Mix for **30 sec/reverse stir/speed 1**. Spoon the mixture over the vegetables and serve hot.

SERVING SUGGESTIONS
Serve with Almond brown basmati pilaf (page 158) or Cauliflower and sweet potato smash (page 163).

DAIRY-FREE | GLUTEN-FREE | PALEO

CHICKEN BOLOGNESE

For some reason, bolognese in our household is always much better received when it's made with chicken instead of beef. In summer we have it served over raw vegetable noodles and in winter it often gets dolloped over a lovely bowl of steaming mashed potato.

SERVES 4
Preparation time 5 minutes
Cooking time 25 minutes

2 garlic cloves
2 celery stalks, cut into 5 cm (2 inch) lengths
1 carrot, cut into 3
1 onion, peeled and quartered
2 tomatoes, cored and quartered
2 teaspoons dried mixed herbs
50 g (1¾ oz) butter
500 g (1 lb 2 oz) minced (ground) chicken
60 g (2 oz/½ cup) Tomato mix (page 28)
1 tablespoon Stock 'cube' of choice (pages 34–5)

Chop the garlic, celery, carrot, onion and tomato for **5 sec/speed 7**. Scrape down the side of the bowl. Add the dried mixed herbs, butter and minced chicken. Cook for **10 min/ 100°C/reverse stir/speed 1**.

Add the tomato mix, stock cube and 80 ml (2½ fl oz/⅓ cup) water. Cook for **15 min/ 100°C/reverse stir/speed 1**. Serve hot.

SERVING SUGGESTIONS
Spoon over your favourite cooked wholemeal (whole-wheat) pasta, rice, spelt or kelp noodles or over raw spiral vegetable noodles (use a spiraliser tool to make these yourself at home).

GLUTEN-FREE | NUT-FREE | PALEO

STICKY PORK

Yummy, sticky, finger-licking pork spare ribs. Finishing these bad boys off in the oven just takes it up a notch but, if you are strapped for time, they are still gorgeous just cooked in the mixer. They are versatile, too, as you can serve them either with Mexican or Asian-flavoured side dishes – I personally like them with the Cauliflower and sweet potato smash (page 163).

SERVES 4

Preparation time 5 minutes
Cooking time 40 minutes

2 teaspoons sweet paprika
2 tablespoons pure maple syrup
80 ml (2½ fl oz/⅓ cup) apple cider vinegar
1 Stock 'cube' of choice (pages 34–5)
1 tablespoon Tomato mix (page 28)
2 tablespoons tamari (gluten-free soy sauce)
6 pork belly spare ribs, total weight 950 g (2 lb 2 oz),
    bone removed, each cut into 3 crossways

Mix the paprika, maple syrup, vinegar, stock cube, 80 ml (2½ fl oz/ ⅓ cup) water, the tomato mix and the tamari for **10 sec/speed 5**.

Add the pork belly pieces. Attach the steaming bowl, instead of the measuring cup, to the mixer bowl lid. Cook for **25 min/steam mode/ reverse stir/speed 1**.

Meanwhile, preheat the oven to 200°C (400°F)/180°C (350°F) fan-forced. Line a large baking tray with baking paper.

Add the pork and sauce to the tray in a single layer. Bake for 15 minutes or until the pork caramelises and the sauce thickens. Serve hot.

DAIRY-FREE | GLUTEN-FREE | NUT-FREE | PALEO

ALL-IN-ONE TIP

Throw some chopped vegetables into the steaming bowl attachment and place it on top of the pork while it's cooking.

POACHED CHICKEN WITH GINGER OIL

This is my cheat's version of Hainanese chicken. All the same flavour combinations are present, but the ingredients used make this a much faster preparation and cooking method.

SERVES 4

Preparation time 10 minutes
Cooking time 25 minutes

4 spring onions (scallions), cut into 4 cm (1½ inch) lengths,
    plus 2 extra spring onions, halved
4 cm (1½ inch) piece fresh ginger, peeled, plus
    5 cm (2 inch) extra, sliced
80 ml (2½ fl oz/⅓ cup) Garlic frying oil (page 21)
1 teaspoon sesame oil, plus 2 teaspoons extra
6 small skinless chicken thigh fillets, total weight
    650 g (1 lb 7 oz), halved crossways
1 tablespoon Stock 'cube' of choice (pages 34–5)
coriander (cilantro) leaves, to serve
sliced red chilli, to serve
lime wedges, to serve

Chop the spring onion and ginger for **3 sec/speed 5**. Scrape down the side of the bowl. Chop again for **3 sec/speed 5**. Scrape down the side of the bowl.

Add the frying oil and cook for **5 minutes/120°C/reverse stir/speed 1**.

Transfer the mixture to a heatproof bowl. Stir in the sesame oil and set aside.

Add the chicken, stock cube, 750 ml (26 fl oz/3 cups) water, the extra spring onion, extra ginger and extra sesame oil. Cook for **20 min/100°C/ reverse stir/speed 1**.

Transfer the chicken to serving bowls. Spoon over a little of the poaching liquid. Serve hot, topped with the coriander and chilli, the reserved ginger oil for dipping and the lime for squeezing.

DAIRY-FREE | GLUTEN-FREE | NUT-FREE | PALEO

SERVING SUGGESTIONS

Steamed Asian greens (page 153), Almond brown basmati pilaf (page 158).

SOUTHERN-STYLE CHICKEN FINGERS

My very own version of crispy crumbed chicken. The children devour these every time, which is always satisfying to see.

SERVES 4

Preparation time 10 minutes
Cooking time 16 minutes

115 g (4 oz/½ cup) popping corn kernels
55 g (2 oz/¼ cup) whole wheat grains (see Note page 45)
1 tablespoon sweet paprika
3 teaspoons garlic powder
3 teaspoons onion powder
2 eggs
600 g (1 lb 5 oz) chicken tenderloins
Garlic frying oil (page 21), for cooking

Mill the popping corn kernels and wheat grains for **30 sec/speed 10**. Scrape down the side of the bowl.

Add the paprika, garlic powder and onion powder. Mix for **5 sec/speed 5**. Transfer the spice mixture to a large plate.

Whisk the eggs in a flat bowl. Add the chicken, turning to coat well on all sides. Dip the chicken into the spice mixture, turning to coat well on all sides.

Preheat a large frying pan over medium heat. Add a little oil to coat the base of the pan. Add the chicken and cook, in batches, turning occasionally, for 8 minutes or until cooked through and golden.

DAIRY-FREE | NUT-FREE

SERVING SUGGESTIONS

Smoky avo mayo (see page 26), Simple buttery veg (page 166), mashed potatoes.

SALSA CHICKEN

If you can, try to use super-ripe tomatoes for the salsa mix for added flavour and sweetness – either roma (plum) or vine-ripened varieties are great. You can serve the mixture with Spinach and corn tortillas (page 68), spooned over rice or on top of nachos.

SERVES 4

Preparation time 7 minutes
Cooking time 40 minutes

2 garlic cloves
1 red onion, peeled and quartered
2 coriander (cilantro) sprigs, including the stems and roots,
   well washed and torn in half
500 g (1 lb 2 oz) ripe red tomatoes, cored and quartered
1 red capsicum (pepper), seeded and cut into 8
1 tablespoon Tomato mix (page 28)
1 tablespoon apple cider vinegar
3 teaspoons ground cumin
3 teaspoons sweet paprika
1 tablespoon Stock 'cube' of choice (pages 34–5)
1 tablespoon pure maple syrup
500 g (1 lb 2 oz) skinless chicken thigh fillets

Blend the garlic, onion, coriander, tomato, capsicum, tomato mix, vinegar, cumin, paprika, stock cube and maple syrup for **30 sec/speed 7**. Scrape down the side of the bowl.

Add the chicken and cook for **40 min/100°C/reverse stir/speed 1**.

Shred the mixture for **3 sec/reverse stir/speed 4**. Serve hot.

DAIRY-FREE | GLUTEN-FREE | NUT-FREE | PALEO

SERVING SUGGESTION

Adorn with all the usual favourites – sliced avocado, lime wedges, coriander (cilantro) leaves and a dollop of Cow's milk yoghurt (page 14).

BEEF AND LAMB

MEATBALLS IN MUSTARD SAUCE

I live very close to one of those large, yellow-coloured Swedish home stores where lots of people rave about a dish prepared in their restaurant. Personally, I've never understood the attraction. However, with this off-the-beaten-track version, I totally get it.

SERVES 4
Preparation time 15 minutes
Cooking time 22 minutes

1 brown onion, peeled and quartered
250 g (9 oz) minced (ground) beef
300 g (10½ oz) minced (ground) pork
½ teaspoon freshly grated nutmeg
½ teaspoon ground white pepper
2 tablespoons Garlic frying oil (page 21), plus 1 tablespoon extra
1 tablespoon yellow mustard seeds
½ teaspoon ground turmeric
1 tablespoon Stock 'cube' of choice (pages 34–5)
250 ml (9 fl oz/1 cup) cream of choice (cow's or coconut)
2 tablespoons dill leaf tips
1 tablespoon chopped chives

Chop the onion for **5 sec/speed 4**. Scrape down the side of the bowl. Transfer half the onion to a bowl and set aside.

Add the minced beef and pork, nutmeg and pepper to the onion in the mixer bowl. Mix for **20 sec/speed 5**.

Shape 1 tablespoon measures of the meat mixture into balls and set aside.

Heat the oil in a large frying pan over medium heat. Add the meatballs and cook, turning occasionally, for 12 minutes or until cooked and golden. Remove from the heat and cover to keep warm.

Meanwhile, return the reserved onion to the mixer bowl. Add the mustard seeds, turmeric and extra oil. Cook for **5 min/120°C/reverse stir/speed 1**. Scrape down the side of the bowl.

Add the stock cube and cream. Cook for **5 min/100°C/reverse stir/speed 1**.

Add the mustard sauce, dill and chives to the meatballs in the frying pan and toss gently to combine. Serve hot.

GLUTEN-FREE | NUT-FREE

PAPRIKA LAMB HOT POT

My Russian grandmother, or 'Baba', would make the most delicious paprika lamb dish for Saturday lunch. I have tried hard to re-create her legendary dish and this one comes pretty darn close.

SERVES 4

Preparation time 10 minutes
Cooking time 24 minutes

2 tablespoons Garlic frying oil (page 21), plus 1 tablespoon extra
2 brown onions, thinly sliced
1 large red capsicum (pepper), thinly sliced
2 teaspoons pure maple syrup
1 tablespoon red wine vinegar
400 g (14 oz) lamb backstraps (loin fillets), thinly sliced
1 teaspoon caraway seeds
1½ tablespoons sweet paprika
1 tablespoon Tomato mix (page 28)
1 tablespoon Stock 'cube' of choice (pages 34–5)
2 tomatoes, chopped
1 small handful flat-leaf (Italian) parsley leaves

Cook the oil, onion, capsicum, maple syrup and vinegar for **5 min/ steam mode/reverse stir/soft stir**. Scrape down the side of the bowl. Cook for **5 min/steam mode/reverse stir/soft stir**.

Meanwhile, preheat a large frying pan over high heat. Combine the lamb and extra oil in a bowl. Brown the lamb in the pan, in two separate batches, for 3 minutes each. Transfer the meat to a heatproof plate and cover to keep warm.

Add 185 ml (6 fl oz/¾ cup) water to the same pan. Bring to the boil, scraping all the flavourings from the base of the pan. Set aside.

Add the caraway seeds, paprika, tomato mix, stock cube and tomato to the onion mixture in the mixer bowl. Cook for **3 min/120°C/reverse stir/ speed 1**.

Add the browned lamb and the water mixture. Attach the simmering basket, instead of the measuring cup, to the mixer bowl lid. Cook for **5 min/120°C/reverse stir/soft stir**. Serve hot.

DAIRY-FREE | GLUTEN-FREE | NUT-FREE | PALEO

SERVING SUGGESTIONS

Cow's milk yoghurt (page 14), mashed potatoes, Almond brown basmati pilaf (page 158).

BEEF BOURGUIGNON

This is literally the only dish I ever cook that has added alcohol. Don't worry, though – the cooking time means that all the alcohol vaporises away, leaving you with just the lovely rich flavour of the wine (so use a good-quality one).

SERVES 4

Preparation time 10 minutes
Cooking time 2 hours

600 g (1 lb 5 oz) chopped stewing beef (chuck or gravy beef)
1 tablespoon Garlic frying oil (page 21), plus 1 tablespoon extra
125 ml (4 fl oz/½ cup) red wine
1 red onion, cut into wedges
4 rashers rindless streaky bacon, thickly sliced crossways
2 tablespoons Tomato mix (page 28)
1 tablespoon Stock 'cube' of choice (pages 34–5)
200 g (7 oz) small button mushrooms
baby English spinach leaves, to serve

Preheat a large frying pan over high heat. Combine the beef and oil in a bowl, turning to coat the meat.

Brown the beef in the pan, in two separate batches, for 3 minutes each. Transfer to a heatproof plate and set aside.

Add the wine to the same pan. Bring to the boil and cook, scraping all the flavourings from the base of the pan, for 3 minutes or until the mixture reduces by half. Set aside.

Meanwhile, place the onion, bacon and the extra oil in the mixer bowl. Attach the simmering basket, instead of the measuring cup, to the mixer bowl lid. Cook for **5 min/120°C/reverse stir/soft stir**.

Add the tomato mix, stock cube, 250 ml (9 fl oz/1 cup) water, the browned beef and the reduced wine mixture. Cook for **99 min/90°C/reverse stir/soft stir**.

Remove the simmering basket from the lid. Add the mushrooms. Cook for **10 min/120°C/reverse stir/soft stir**. Serve hot with the baby English spinach leaves.

See photograph on pages 110–11.

DAIRY-FREE | GLUTEN-FREE | NUT-FREE | PALEO

SERVING SUGGESTIONS

French-dressed Lentils (page 172), Simple buttery veg (page 166).

BEEF BOURGUIGNON (PAGE 108)

LAMB MASSAMAN

A great introduction to eating Thai food is to sit down to a bowl of massaman curry. Although normally made with beef, I use lamb instead as it gives an added flavour boost.

SERVES 4

Preparation time 10 minutes
Cooking time 55 minutes

2 tablespoons Garlic frying oil (page 21)
55 g (2 oz/¼ cup) Asian paste (page 32)
1 teaspoon ground cinnamon
¼ teaspoon ground cloves
¼ teaspoon ground white pepper
1 red onion, cut into thin wedges
400 g (14 oz) lamb backstraps (loin fillets), cut into
    2 cm (¾ inch) pieces
250 ml (9 fl oz/1 cup) Coconut cream (page 17)
125 ml (4 fl oz/½ cup) Coconut milk (page 17)
500 g (1 lb 2 oz) baby red-skinned potatoes, quartered
1 teaspoon pure maple syrup
2 teaspoons tamari (gluten-free soy sauce)
coriander (cilantro) leaves, to serve
lime wedges, to serve

Cook the oil, Asian paste, cinnamon, ground cloves and pepper for **5 min/120°C/speed 1**. Scrape down the side of the bowl.

Add the onion and lamb. Cook for **10 min/120°C/reverse stir/speed 1**. Scrape down the side of the bowl.

Add the coconut cream and coconut milk. Cook for **30 min/100°C/reverse stir/speed 1**.

Add the potato, maple syrup and tamari. Cook for **10 min/100°C/reverse stir/speed 1**. Serve hot, topped with the coriander leaves and with the lime wedges for squeezing.

DAIRY-FREE | GLUTEN-FREE | NUT-FREE

MADRAS BEEF

Who doesn't love a good curry? This fuss-free and very speedy version has all the depth of flavour of a traditional version and certainly surpasses any take-away or store-bought jar variety.

SERVES 4

Preparation time 10 minutes
Cooking time 23 minutes

1 tablespoon coriander seeds
3 teaspoons cumin seeds
½ teaspoon dried chilli flakes (optional)
2 garlic cloves
1 brown onion, peeled and quartered
3 cm (1¼ inch) piece fresh ginger, peeled
3 cm (1¼ inch) piece fresh turmeric, peeled
50 g (1¾ oz) butter, chopped
1 tablespoon Stock 'cube' of choice (pages 34–5)
40 g (1½ oz/⅓ cup) Tomato mix (page 28)
600 g (1 lb 5 oz) rump steak, cut into 3 cm (1¼ inch) pieces
Cow's milk yoghurt (page 14), to serve
coriander (cilantro) leaves, to serve

Mill the coriander seeds, cumin seeds and chilli flakes, if using, for **1 min/speed 9**. Scrape down the side of the bowl.

Add the garlic, onion, ginger and turmeric. Chop for **5 sec/speed 7**. Scrape down the side of the bowl.

Add the butter and cook for **3 min/100°C/speed 1**.

Add the stock cube and tomato mix, 185 ml (6 fl oz/¾ cup) water and the steak. Cook for **20 min/100°C/reverse stir/speed 1**. Serve topped with the yoghurt and coriander leaves.

GLUTEN-FREE | NUT-FREE

SERVING SUGGESTIONS

Almond brown basmati pilaf (page 158), Raw rainbow vegetable 'rice' (page 160).

CHUNKY BEEF PIE

Family pies are the best. The filling in this one is so hearty that I defy anyone who says otherwise. The pastry top adds the perfect buttery crunch that we all love, yet it's completely gluten-free.

SERVES 6

Preparation time 15 minutes
Cooking time 1 hour 20 minutes

1 red onion, peeled and quartered
2 garlic cloves
1 tablespoon rosemary leaves
200 g (7 oz) button mushrooms
50 g (1¾ oz) butter
700 g (1 lb 9 oz) rump steak, cut into 2 cm (¾ inch) pieces
1 tablespoon Stock 'cube' of choice (pages 34–5)
30 g (1 oz/¼ cup) Tomato mix (page 28), plus extra to serve
250 ml (9 fl oz/1 cup) water
1 quantity Macadamia pastry (page 22)
1 egg, whisked

Place the onion, garlic, rosemary and mushrooms in the mixer bowl. Chop for **3 sec/speed 7**. Scrape down the side of the bowl.

Add the butter and cook for **5 min/120°C/speed 1**. Scrape down the side of the bowl. Add the beef and cook for **5 min/120°C/reverse stir/speed 1**.

Add all the remaining ingredients. Attach the simmering basket, instead of the measuring cup, to the mixer bowl lid. Cook for **45 min/100°C/ reverse stir/soft stir**.

Pour the mixture into a 24 cm (9½ inch) round pie dish. Leave to stand to cool slightly.

Preheat the oven to 200°C (400°F)/180°C (350°F) fan-forced.

Roll out the pastry between two sheets of baking paper to a 5 mm (¼ inch) thick, 24 cm (9½ inch) diameter disc. Carefully transfer this pastry lid to the top of the beef mixture in the pie dish. Don't worry if it cracks or breaks; simply press it back together again. Trim and discard the excess pastry and brush the top with the whisked egg. Bake for 25 minutes or until the crust is cooked and golden.

GLUTEN-FREE | PALEO

KOREAN BEEF

Another super-easy and quick dinner, this is my twist on the tradition Korean bulgolgi beef.

SERVES 4

Preparation time 5 minutes
Cooking time 20 minutes

4 spring onions (scallions), cut into 4 cm (1½ inch) lengths,
   plus extra sliced spring onion
2 garlic cloves
4 cm (1½ inch) piece fresh ginger, peeled and halved
1 tablespoon Garlic frying oil (page 21)
1 large pinch dried chilli flakes (optional)
500 g (1 lb 2 oz) minced (ground) beef
1 teaspoon sesame oil
60 ml (2 fl oz/¼ cup) tamari (gluten-free soy sauce)
toasted sesame seeds, to serve

Chop the spring onion, garlic and ginger for **5 sec/speed 5**. Scrape down the side of the bowl.

Add the garlic frying oil and cook for **5 min/120°C/speed 1**. Scrape down the side of the bowl.

Add the chilli flakes, if using, and beef. Cook for **10 min/120°C/reverse stir/speed 1**. Scrape down the side of the bowl.

Add the sesame oil and tamari. Attach the simmering basket, instead of the measuring cup, to the mixer bowl lid. Cook for **5 min/120°C/reverse stir/speed 1**. Serve sprinkled with the toasted sesame seeds.

DAIRY-FREE | GLUTEN-FREE | NUT-FREE | PALEO

SERVING SUGGESTIONS

Korean steamed eggplant (page 152), Almond brown basmati pilaf (page 158).

BEEF AND LAMB KOFTA

So versatile and so tasty – you can shape these into mini meatballs, large patties or even just pan-fry the minced (ground) mixture. Whether fried, barbecued or baked, these tasty morsels are perfect year-round and happily fill everyone's bellies.

SERVES 4

Preparation time 15 minutes
Cooking time 8 minutes

4 spring onions (scallions), cut into 4 cm (1½ inch) lengths
1 large handful flat-leaf (Italian) parsley leaves
200 g (7 oz) cauliflower florets
2 garlic cloves
2 teaspoons ground cumin
2 teaspoons ground coriander
1 teaspoon ground cinnamon
2 teaspoons sea salt
1 teaspoon ground white pepper
300 g (10½ oz) minced (ground) beef
250 g (9 oz) minced (ground) lamb

Chop the spring onion, parsley, cauliflower and garlic for **20 sec/ speed 5**. Scrape down the side of the bowl. Chop for **5 sec/speed 5**. Scrape down the side of the bowl.

Add all the remaining ingredients and mix for **20 sec/speed 5**.

Shape 2 tablespoon measures of the mixture firmly into 8 cm (3¼ inch) long sausage shapes.

Preheat a large chargrill pan over medium heat. Cook the kofta sausages for 8 minutes, turning occasionally, or until cooked through and golden.

DAIRY-FREE | GLUTEN-FREE | NUT-FREE | PALEO

SEAFOOD

PRAWN AND PORK SAN CHOY BAU

This is absolutely the most fun you can have at dinnertime. I usually just place the lettuce leaves, prawn and pork mixture and the toppings in the centre of the table and let everyone build their own.

SERVES 4

Preparation time 10 minutes
Cooking time 8 minutes

1 small iceberg lettuce, leaves separated
50 g (1¾ oz) baby kale leaves
4 spring onions (scallions), cut into 4 cm (1½ inch) lengths
2 celery stalks, cut into 4 cm (1½ inch) lengths
2 garlic cloves
4 cm (1½ inch) piece fresh ginger, peeled
1 teaspoon sesame oil
200 g (7 oz) minced (ground) pork
300 g (10½ oz) peeled, deveined raw banana or tiger prawns (shrimp)
2 tablespoons tamari (gluten-free soy sauce)
60 g (2¼ oz/½ cup) mixed salad sprouts

Divide the iceberg lettuce leaves among four serving plates. Fill the lettuce leaves with the baby kale leaves and set aside.

Chop the spring onion, celery, garlic and ginger for **5 sec/speed 5**. Scrape down the side of the bowl.

Add the oil, pork, prawn meat and tamari. Attach the simmering basket, instead of the measuring cup, to the mixer bowl lid. Cook for **8 min/100°C/reverse stir/soft stir**.

Spoon the mixture into the lettuce leaves and top with the salad sprouts. Serve hot.

DAIRY-FREE | GLUTEN-FREE | NUT-FREE | PALEO

NOTE
If you are unable to find baby kale leaves, then just tear two large kale leaves into 3 cm (1¼ inch) pieces.

FISH WITH TOMATO SAUCE

This is a great dish for children who are tasting fish for the first time as the fish is so delicate and sweet tasting and is served with a perfect tomato sauce. You could also serve it with some cooked brown rice, steamed vegies or crispy salad.

SERVES 4

Preparation time 10 minutes
Cooking time 20 minutes

1 red onion, peeled and quartered
1 carrot, cut into 3
1 zucchini (courgette), cut into 3
1 garlic clove
50 g (1¾ oz) butter, chopped
1 tablespoon Stock 'cube' of choice (pages 34–5)
2 tablespoons Tomato mix (page 28)
500 g (1 lb 2 oz) roma (plum) tomatoes, cored and quartered
500 g (1 lb 2 oz) skinless, boneless white fish fillets,
    such as whiting or bream, cut into 2 cm (¾ inch) pieces
flat-leaf (Italian) parsley leaves, to serve
small basil leaves, to serve

Chop the onion, carrot, zucchini and garlic for **30 sec/speed 5**. Scrape down the side of the bowl.

Add the butter and cook for **5 min/120°C/speed 1**. Scrape down the side of the bowl.

Add the stock cube, tomato mix, tomato and 125 ml (4 fl oz/½ cup) water. Cook for **10 min/120°C/speed 1**. Blend for **10 sec/speed 5**.

Add the fish. Attach the simmering basket, instead of the measuring cup, to the mixer bowl lid. Cook for **5 minutes/120°C/reverse stir/soft stir**. Serve hot, topped with the parsley and basil.

GLUTEN-FREE | NUT-FREE | PALEO

SERVING
SUGGESTION

Vegetable noodles (use a spiraliser tool to make these yourself at home).

CREAMY SEAFOOD AND VEG GRATIN

The crispy vegetable topping on this gratin really lifts this dish to the next level.

SERVES 4

Preparation time 10 minutes
Cooking time 33 minutes

700 g (1 lb 9 oz) mixed fresh sustainable seafood, such as skinless flathead fillets, peeled and deveined raw banana prawns/shrimp or cleaned, thickly sliced squid
4 zucchini (courgettes), cut into 3
200 g (7 oz) cauliflower florets
1 handful flat-leaf (Italian) parsley leaves
100 g (3½ oz) butter, chopped
2 leeks, white part only, cut into 3 cm (1¼ inch) lengths
2 carrots, cut into 3
1 red onion, peeled and quartered
2 tablespoons French tarragon leaves
1 tablespoon Stock 'cube' of choice (pages 34–5)
250 ml (9 fl oz/1 cup) cream of choice (cow's or coconut)

Preheat the oven to 200°C (400°F)/180°C (350°F) fan-forced. Place the seafood into a 30 x 20 cm (12 x 8 inch) baking dish.

Chop the zucchini, cauliflower and parsley for **3 sec/speed 5**. Scrape down the side of the bowl. Chop again for **3 sec/speed 5**. Transfer to a bowl and set aside.

Melt the butter for **1 min/100°C/speed 1**. Transfer half the butter to the bowl with the zucchini mixture and toss to coat well. Set aside.

Add the leek, carrot, onion and tarragon to the remaining butter in the mixer bowl. Chop for **5 sec/speed 7**. Cook for **10 min/100°C/speed 1**. Scrape down the side of the bowl.

Add the stock cube and cream. Attach the simmering basket, instead of the measuring cup, to the mixer bowl lid. Cook for **2 min/90°C/speed 1**.

Pour the sauce over the seafood in the dish. Sprinkle the top evenly with the zucchini mixture. Bake for 20 minutes or until the seafood is cooked and the top golden. Serve hot.

GLUTEN-FREE | NUT-FREE

GREEN RISOTTO WITH CALAMARI

This is a dish worthy of a dinner party, but the beauty is that your all-in-one mixer does all the hard work of stirring the risotto while you get to relax.

SERVES 4

Preparation time 5 minutes
Cooking time 63 minutes

1 brown onion, peeled and quartered
1 celery stalk, cut into 4 cm (1½ inch) lengths
2 garlic cloves
40 g (1½ oz) butter, chopped, plus 20 g (¾ oz) extra
250 g (9 oz) medium-grain brown rice, rinsed
2 tablespoons Stock 'cube' of choice (pages 34–5)
100 g (3½ oz) baby English spinach leaves
85 g (3 oz/⅓ cup) Super-greens pesto (page 25)
2 tablespoons Garlic frying oil (page 21)
500 g (1 lb 2 oz) raw baby calamari, cleaned, tentacles reserved, thickly sliced into rings
lemon wedges, to serve

Chop the onion, celery and garlic for **5 sec/speed 5**. Scrape down the side of the bowl. Add the butter and cook for **5 min/100°C/speed 1**. Scrape down the side of the bowl.

Add the rice, stock cube and 1 litre (35 fl oz/4 cups) water. Attach the simmering basket, instead of the measuring cup, to the mixer bowl lid. Cook for **55 min/100°C/reverse stir/speed 1**.

Transfer the mixture to a large heatproof bowl. Add the spinach and pesto and stir gently to combine. Set aside, covered, for 5 minutes.

Meanwhile, heat the oil and extra butter in a large frying pan over medium–high heat. Add the calamari and cook, tossing, for 2–3 minutes or until just cooked and light golden.

Serve the hot risotto topped with the calamari and lemon wedges.

See photograph on pages 124–5.

GLUTEN-FREE

GREEN RISOTTO WITH
CALAMARI (PAGE 122)

MOROCCAN FISH STEW

This is a dish that transcends seasons for me. In the cooler months I love serving bowls of the stew with Cauliflower focaccia (page 164), and in the warmer months I like spooning it over a bowl of Raw rainbow vegetable 'rice' (page 160).

SERVES 4

Preparation time 5 minutes
Cooking time 12 minutes

4 garlic cloves
1 bunch coriander (cilantro), cut into 4 cm (1½ inch) lengths
60 ml (2 fl oz/¼ cup) Garlic frying oil (page 21)
½ teaspoon dried chilli flakes
3 teaspoons ground turmeric
1 tablespoon sweet paprika
2 carrots, sliced
1 red capsicum (pepper), sliced
1 tablespoon Stock 'cube' of choice (pages 34–5)
500 g (1 lb 2 oz) skinless, boneless fish, such as mackerel or trevally, cut into 3 cm (1¼ inch) pieces
coriander (cilantro) leaves, to serve
lemon wedges, to serve

Chop the garlic and coriander for **5 sec/speed 5**. Scrape down the side of the bowl.

Add the oil, chilli, turmeric and paprika. Cook for **2 min/100°C/speed 1**.

Add the carrot, capsicum, stock cube and 250 ml (9 fl oz/1 cup) water. Cook for **5 min/100°C/reverse stir/soft stir**.

Add the fish. Attach the simmering basket, instead of the measuring cup, to the mixer bowl lid. Cook for **5 min/100°C/reverse stir/soft stir**. Serve hot with the coriander leaves and lemon wedges.

DAIRY-FREE | GLUTEN-FREE | NUT-FREE | PALEO

SALT AND PEPPER PRAWNS

These guys are so finger-licking good that you will need to ration them out. Serve them alongside a Vietnamese salad (page 149) and some brown rice.

SERVES 4

Preparation time 5 minutes
Cooking time 12 minutes

50 g (1¾ oz/¼ cup) tapioca pearls
2 teaspoons sea salt
1 teaspoon ground white pepper
1 teaspoon Chinese five spice
500 g (1 lb 2 oz) raw, peeled, deveined tiger prawns (shrimp),
    tails left on
8 French shallots, peeled
2 garlic cloves
1 long red chilli, halved
4 spring onions (scallions), cut into 4 cm (1½ inch) lengths
60 ml (2 fl oz/¼ cup) Garlic frying oil (page 21),
    plus 60 ml (2 fl oz/¼ cup) extra
lime wedges, to serve

Mill the tapioca, sea salt, pepper and five spice for **30 sec/speed 9**. Transfer to a large plate. Add the prawns to this mixture, turning to coat well on all sides. Set aside.

Chop the golden shallots, garlic, chilli and spring onion for **5 sec/speed 7**. Scrape down the side of the bowl.

Add the oil. Attach the simmering basket, instead of the measuring cup, to the mixer bowl lid. Cook for **5 min/120°C/speed 1**. Transfer the mixture to a heatproof bowl.

Heat the extra oil in a large frying pan over medium–high heat. Cook the prawns in the pan, turning occasionally, for 7 minutes or until just cooked and golden. Add the chilli mixture and gently toss to coat the prawns. Serve hot with the lime wedges.

DAIRY-FREE | GLUTEN-FREE | NUT-FREE | PALEO

CRISPY FLATHEAD

This 50-second batter is the lightest, crispiest batter you will ever taste. Children will devour this fish and adults will love it served with some Tartare avo mayo (see page 26) for dipping.

SERVES 4

Preparation time 5 minutes
Cooking time 6 minutes

150 g (5½ oz/¾ cup) brown basmati rice
100 g (3½ oz/½ cup) tapioca pearls
2 teaspoons sea salt
½ teaspoon ground white pepper
8 skinless flathead fillets (or bream or whiting)
250 ml (9 fl oz/1 cup) chilled sparkling water
1 chilled egg
coconut oil or macadamia oil, for cooking
lemon wedges, to serve

Mill the rice, tapioca, salt and pepper for **1 min/speed 10**. Scrape down the side of the bowl.

Transfer 3 tablespoons of the mixture to a large plate. Add the fish to the mixture, turning to coat lightly on all sides. Set aside.

Add the sparkling water and egg to the remaining mixture in the mixer bowl. Blend for **20 sec/speed 4**. Scrape down the side of the bowl.

Place enough oil in a deep frying pan to reach a depth of 1 cm (½ inch). Heat over medium–high heat. Once the oil is hot, dip the fish in the batter mixture in the mixer bowl to coat. Allow any excess to drip away, then carefully lower the fish into the hot oil. Cook, turning once, for 6 minutes or until cooked and golden. Serve hot with the lemon wedges.

DAIRY-FREE | GLUTEN-FREE

SERVING SUGGESTIONS

Mushy peas (page 170), Fennel remoulade (page 175), Avo mayo (page 26), Quick pickled vegies (page 150), Cauliflower and sweet potato smash (page 163).

FISH AND VEGIE PATTIES

Here's a children's meal that's a winner with parents, too. If you have any leftovers, the patties are delicious broken up and tossed through a salad the next day for lunch.

MAKES 12

Preparation time 15 minutes
Cooking time 27 minutes + chilling

½ bunch chives, cut into 5 cm (2 inch) lengths
1 zucchini (courgette), cut into 3
1 carrot, cut into 3
600 g (1 lb 5 oz) floury potatoes, peeled and cut into
    2 cm (¾ inch) pieces
80 ml (2½ fl oz/⅓ cup) milk
150 g (5½ oz) skinless, boneless white fish fillets, such as bream
    or whiting, cut into 3 cm (1¼ inch) pieces
1 egg
Garlic frying oil (page 21), for cooking

Chop the chives, zucchini and carrot for **10 sec/speed 7**. Scrape down the side of the bowl.

Insert the whisk attachment into the mixer bowl. Add the potato and milk. Attach the simmering basket, instead of the measuring cup, to the mixer bowl lid. Cook for **20 min/95°C/speed 1**. Remove the simmering basket from the lid.

Add the fish through the hole in the lid of the bowl. Use a spatula through the hole to make sure the fish falls away from the inserted whisk attachment and into the potato mixture in the bowl. Attach the simmering basket to the mixer bowl lid. Cook for **5 min/95°C/speed 1**. Mix for **30 sec/speed 3**.

Transfer the mixture to a bowl and set aside to cool slightly, then chill for 2 hours or until firm. Stir in the egg until well combined.

Heat the oil in a large frying pan over medium–high heat. Drop 60 ml (2 fl oz/¼ cup) measures of the mixture into the pan. Cook the patties for 1–2 minutes each side or until golden. Serve warm.

GLUTEN-FREE | NUT-FREE

SERVING SUGGESTIONS

For children, serve with yoghurt or Avo mayo (page 26) for dipping. For adults, serve with Espresso barbecue sauce (page 27) or Smoky avo mayo (page 26) for dipping.

CAULIFLOWER 'STEAKS' WITH SATAY SAUCE

This is one of the most filling meals you will ever try. I adore cauliflower in all forms but especially when it's baked to a golden crisp – so moreish and simple.

SERVES 4

Preparation time 5 minutes
Cooking time 25 minutes

2 x 500 g (1 lb 2 oz) whole cauliflowers, each cut into 4 thick slices
60 ml (2 fl oz/¼ cup) Garlic frying oil (page 21)
110 g (3¾ oz/¾ cup) salted, roasted peanuts, plus extra, chopped, to serve
1 tablespoon Asian paste (page 32)
2 teaspoons pure maple syrup
1 tablespoon lime juice
500 ml (17 fl oz/2 cups) Coconut cream (page 17)
coriander (cilantro) leaves, to serve
Thai basil leaves, to serve
lime wedges, to serve

Preheat the oven to 220°C (425°F)/200°C (400°F) fan-forced. Line two large baking trays with baking paper.

Place the cauliflower steaks on the prepared trays. Brush both sides with some of the oil. Bake for 20–25 minutes or until cooked and golden.

Meanwhile, cook the peanuts, Asian paste, maple syrup, lime juice, coconut cream and remaining oil for **5 min/100°C/speed 1**. Blend **1 min/speed 5**, slowly increasing to **speed 9**.

Divide the cauliflower steaks among four serving plates. Spoon over the satay sauce. Top with the coriander, Thai basil, extra chopped peanuts and lime wedges. Serve hot.

DAIRY-FREE | GLUTEN-FREE | VEGAN | VEGETARIAN

LENTIL COTTAGE PIE

This is a great make-and-take dish and perfect through the cooler months. All you need are some steamed greens to serve alongside the pie, and you have a very filling meal.

SERVES 4

Preparation time 10 minutes
Cooking time 47 minutes

700 g (1 lb 9 oz) sweet potatoes, skins scrubbed, cut into
    2 cm (¾ inch) pieces
50 g (1¾ oz) butter, chopped, plus an extra 50 g (1¾ oz)
2 carrots, cut into 3
2 celery stalks, cut into 4 cm (1½ inch) lengths
2 zucchini (courgettes), cut into 3
1 tablespoon Stock 'cube' of choice (pages 34–5)
2 tablespoons Tomato mix (page 28)
400 g (14 oz/2 cups) cooked French blue-green lentils
    (see page 37)
Garlic frying oil (page 21), for brushing

Add 500 ml (17 fl oz/2 cups) water to the mixer bowl. Attach the steaming bowl, instead of the measuring cup, to the mixer bowl lid. Add the sweet potato to the steaming bowl and cover with the lid. Cook for **20 min/steam mode/speed 2**.

Transfer the sweet potato to a heatproof bowl, add the butter, and crush the sweet potato lightly with a fork. Set aside.

Chop the carrot, celery and zucchini for **5 sec/speed 5**. Scrape down the side of the bowl. Add the extra butter and cook for **10 min/120°C/ speed 1**.

Add the stock cube, tomato mix, lentils and 125 ml (4 fl oz/½ cup) water. Cook for **10 min/100°C/speed 1**.

Transfer the mixture to a 1.5 litre (52 fl oz/6 cup) capacity baking dish. Top with the crushed sweet potato. Brush the top of the sweet potato with oil.

Preheat a stove grill (broiler) to high. Grill (broil) the pie for 5–7 minutes or until the sweet potato is crisp and golden. Serve hot.

GLUTEN-FREE | NUT-FREE | VEGETARIAN

VEGAN MUSHROOM 'PIZZAS'

These are so hearty as a main meal but be sure to serve them with loads of extra greens. These 'pizzas' can also easily feed eight as a brunch or lunch dish, too.

SERVES 4

Preparation time 5 minutes
Cooking time 8 minutes

8 large field mushrooms, stems removed, wiped clean
80 ml (2½ fl oz/⅓ cup) Garlic frying oil (page 21)
4 spring onions (scallions), cut into 4 cm (1½ inch) lengths
2 garlic cloves
1 tablespoon rosemary leaves
3 tablespoons oregano leaves
1 handful basil leaves
170 ml (5½ fl oz/⅔ cup) Nut cream (page 15)
4 tomatoes, sliced

Preheat the oven to 220°C (425°F)/200°C (400°F) fan-forced. Line two large baking trays with baking paper.

Place the mushrooms on the prepared baking trays, cup sides facing up.

Blend the oil, spring onion, garlic, rosemary, oregano and basil for **20 sec/speed 7**. Brush some of the mixture inside each mushroom cup.

Divide the nut cream among the mushrooms, spreading to cover the base of the cups. Top with the sliced tomato. Spoon over the remaining oil mixture. Bake for 8 minutes or until lightly golden. Serve hot.

DAIRY-FREE | GLUTEN-FREE | PALEO | VEGAN | VEGETARIAN

LEMONY BROCCOLI AND FENNEL QUICHE

Here I am paying homage to a recipe I learned to make while in cooking college, more than 22 years ago. The flavour combination of broccoli and lemon in a quiche has always stuck with me, and is a tried and tested crowd pleaser.

SERVES 6

Preparation time 10 minutes
Cooking time 70 minutes + chilling

1 quantity Macadamia pastry (page 22)
6 eggs
125 ml (4 fl oz/½ cup) thin (pouring/whipping) cream
finely grated zest and juice of 1 small lemon
300 g (10½ oz) broccoli, florets separated
25 g (1 oz) butter, chopped
1 baby fennel bulb, trimmed and thinly sliced
115 g (4 oz/½ cup) Fresh ricotta (page 12)
baby English spinach leaves, to serve
baby rocket (arugula) leaves, to serve

Preheat the oven to 180°C (350°F)/160°C (315°F) fan-forced. Place a large baking tray in the oven to preheat. Using your fingertips, press the pastry evenly over the base and side of a 24 cm (9½ inch) glass pie dish. Chill for 30 minutes.

Mix the eggs, cream, lemon zest and juice for **5 sec/speed 5**. Pour the mixture into the pastry shell. Chop the broccoli for **3 sec/speed 4**. Transfer to the egg mixture in the pastry shell.

Cook the butter and fennel for **5 min/120°C/reverse stir/soft stir**. Add this to the egg mixture in the pastry shell, stirring gently to distribute it evenly. Spoon small amounts of ricotta all over the top of the vegetable mixture in the pastry shell. Bake on the preheated tray for 65 minutes, covering loosely with a piece of foil halfway through baking to prevent browning too quickly, or until the egg has just set and the pastry is golden. Leave to cool for 20 minutes in the pie dish before serving warm, topped with the baby spinach and rocket.

GLUTEN-FREE | VEGETARIAN

NOTE
The delicate macadamia pastry will hold its shape but still crumble slightly when warm. For a firmer crust, chill the cooked quiche for 30 minutes.

FALAFEL PATTIES

Crispy on the outside and soft and creamy in the centre – delicious! You can make mini versions of these and serve them as a snack.

SERVES 4

Preparation time 10 minutes
Cooking time 8 minutes

2 garlic cloves
1 bunch flat-leaf (Italian) parsley, torn into 4
1 bunch coriander (cilantro), torn into 4
1 handful mint leaves
1 tablespoon Stock 'cube' of choice (pages 34–5)
3 teaspoons ground cumin
3 teaspoons ground coriander
400 g (14 oz/2 cups) cooked chickpeas (see page 37)
1 egg
80 ml (2½ fl oz/⅓ cup) Garlic frying oil (page 21)

Chop the garlic, parsley, coriander, mint and stock cube for **5 sec/speed 7**. Scrape down the side of the bowl.

Add the cumin, coriander, chickpeas and egg. Mix for **10 sec/speed 6**. Using slightly damp hands, shape the mixture firmly into 12 round patties.

Heat the oil in a large frying pan over medium–high heat. Cook the patties, in batches, for 2 minutes each side or until heated and golden. Serve hot.

GLUTEN-FREE | VEGETARIAN

JAPANESE TOFU AND BROWN RICE BOWLS

What is it about Japanese flavours that just hits the spot? The tofu is so tasty in this recipe and, by all means, if you have a couple of days up your sleeve then marinate it for even longer. For an added level of flavour you can either pan-fry or chargrill the tofu instead of steaming it with the vegies.

SERVES 4

Preparation time 10 minutes
Cooking time 50 minutes

1 teaspoon wasabi paste
2 teaspoons white miso paste
60 ml (2 fl oz/¼ cup) tamari (gluten-free soy sauce)
2 tablespoons lime juice
200 g (7 oz) firm tofu, sliced
400 g (14 oz) medium-grain brown rice
1 tablespoon Stock 'cube' of choice (pages 34–5)
2 bunches asparagus
2 zucchini (courgettes), peeled into long thin strips
    with a vegetable peeler
toasted sesame seeds, to serve

Combine the wasabi, miso paste, tamari and lime juice in a flat dish. Add the tofu, turning to coat it well. Set aside to marinate.

Rinse the rice under cold running water until the water runs clear.

Insert the simmering basket into the mixer bowl. Add the rice, stock cube and 900 ml (31 fl oz) water. Cook for **20 min/100°C/speed 4**. Add an extra 500 ml (17 fl oz/2 cups) water to the mixer bowl. Cook again for **20 min/100°C/speed 4**. Transfer the simmering basket with the rice to a serving bowl, leaving the water in the mixer bowl.

Attach the steaming bowl, instead of the measuring cup, to the mixer bowl lid. Add the asparagus, then the marinated tofu (reserving the marinade) and then the zucchini to the steaming bowl. Attach the steaming bowl lid. Cook for **10 min/steam mode/speed 2**.

Remove the vegetables and tofu.

Divide the rice among four serving bowls. Top with the vegetables and tofu. Spoon over the reserved marinade and sprinkle with the toasted sesame seeds. Serve hot.

GLUTEN-FREE
| VEGAN |
VEGETARIAN

GOLDEN DAL

'Golden bowls of joy' would be another way to describe this warming, hearty, taste sensation.

SERVES 4

Preparation time 10 minutes
Cooking time 47 minutes

4 spring onions (scallions), cut into 4 cm (1½ inch) lengths
2 garlic cloves
2 teaspoons cumin seeds
4 tablespoons small fresh curry leaves
60 ml (2 fl oz/¼ cup) Garlic frying oil (page 21)
1 red onion, peeled and quartered
4 cm (1½ inch) piece fresh turmeric, peeled
2 cm (¾ inch) piece fresh ginger, peeled
2 teaspoons ground cumin
205 g (7¼ oz/1 cup) dried split red lentils
1 tablespoon Stock 'cube' of choice (pages 34–5)
4 baby (patty pan) yellow squash, sliced horizontally through centre
400 g (14 oz) peeled, seeded butternut pumpkin (winter squash), thinly sliced

Chop the spring onion and garlic for **5 sec/speed 5**. Scrape down the side of the bowl.

Add the cumin seeds, curry leaves and oil. Cook for **5 min/120°C/ speed 1**. Transfer to a heatproof bowl but reserve the oil.

Chop the red onion, turmeric and ginger for **20 sec/speed 5**. Scrape down the side of the bowl. Add the cumin and cook for **5 min/120°C/ speed 1**. Scrape down the side of the bowl.

Add the lentils, stock cube and 1 litre (35 fl oz/4 cups) water. Attach the simmering basket, instead of the measuring cup, to the mixer bowl lid. Cook for **30 min/100°C/reverse stir/speed 1**.

Preheat a chargrill pan over high heat. Chargrill the squash and pumpkin for 5–8 minutes or until just cooked and golden.

Divide the dal among four serving bowls. Top with the chargrilled vegetables. Spoon over the curry leaf oil and serve hot.

DAIRY-FREE | GLUTEN-FREE | NUT-FREE | VEGAN | VEGETARIAN

TOFU PENANG CURRY

Unfortunately for me, I am the only person in our household who enjoys eating tofu. So this tasty curry is something I cook for myself when I know I am going to be the only one at home. The leftovers make for a delicious lunch for the next 2 days.

SERVES 4

Preparation time 10 minutes
Cooking time 11 minutes

2 tablespoons Asian paste (page 32)
1 long red chilli, cut into 3
50 g (1¾ oz/⅓ cup) unsalted, roasted peanuts
500 ml (17 fl oz/2 cups) Coconut milk (page 17)
2 teaspoons pure maple syrup
300 g (10½ oz) firm tofu, cut into 3 cm (1¼ inch) pieces
200 g (7 oz) pumpkin (winter squash), peeled, seeded and
     cut into 2 cm (¾ inch) pieces
100 g (3½ oz) sugar snap peas, halved diagonally
Thai basil leaves, to serve
lime wedges, to serve

Chop the Asian paste, chilli and peanuts for **20 sec/speed 7**. Scrape down the side of the bowl.

Add the coconut milk and maple syrup. Cook for **5 min/100°C/ speed 1**. Add the tofu and pumpkin. Cook for **5 min/100°C/reverse stir/speed 1**.

Add the sugar snap peas and cook for **1 min/100°C/reverse stir/speed 1**. Serve with the Thai basil and lime wedges.

DAIRY-FREE | GLUTEN-FREE | VEGAN | VEGETARIAN

SERVING SUGGESTION

Almond brown basmati pilaf (page 158), Raw rainbow vegetable 'rice' (page 160).

KIDNEY BEAN CHILLI

Chilli is my thing and this is just so delicious. It gets even better with age, so if you are able to make it the day before serving, even better. Of course you can completely omit the chilli flakes or add more to suit your family's taste.

SERVES 4

Preparation time 5 minutes
Cooking time 13 minutes

1 brown onion, peeled and quartered
2 garlic cloves
3 teaspoons ground cumin
2 teaspoons sweet paprika
½ teaspoon dried chilli flakes
2 tablespoons Garlic frying oil (page 21)
1 red capsicum (pepper), seeded and chopped
4 tomatoes, cored and chopped
400 g (14 oz/2 cups) cooked red kidney beans (see page 37)
1 handful coriander (cilantro) leaves
1 handful flat-leaf (Italian) parsley leaves
Nut cream (page 15), to serve

Chop the onion and garlic for **10 sec/speed 5**. Scrape down the side of the bowl.

Add the cumin, paprika, chilli and oil. Cook for **3 min/120°C/speed 1**.

Add the capsicum, tomato and beans. Cook for **10 min/100°C/reverse stir/speed 1**.

Add the coriander and parsley. Stir for **20 sec/reverse stir/speed 1**. Serve hot, topped with the nut cream.

DAIRY-FREE | GLUTEN-FREE | VEGAN | VEGETARIAN

simple
sides

GREEN HUMMUS

This hummus gets dolloped on, spooned alongside and is dipped into many kinds of food in our house. The flavour is great but it also looks so lovely, too.

MAKES APPROXIMATELY 440 G (15½ OZ/2 CUPS)

Preparation time 5 minutes

400 g (14 oz/2 cups) cooked chickpeas (see page 37)
100 g (3½ oz) baby English spinach leaves
2 garlic cloves
1 large handful flat-leaf (Italian) parsley leaves
finely grated zest and juice of 1 large lemon
125 ml (4 fl oz/½ cup) avocado oil
1 teaspoon paprika
2 teaspoons sea salt

Blend all the ingredients for **30 sec/speed 9**. Scrape down the side of the bowl.

Blend again for **30 sec/speed 9**. Serve immediately or chill in an airtight container for up to 5 days.

DAIRY-FREE | GLUTEN-FREE | NUT-FREE | VEGAN | VEGETARIAN

MEDITERRANEAN KALE SALAD

Eat this salad on its own or serve it with your favourite main dish. This salad also transports well, so it's great for prepping in the morning and taking to work in an airtight container.

SERVES 4

Preparation time 10 minutes

1 bunch flat-leaf (Italian) parsley, cut into 4 cm (1½ inch) lengths
1 red capsicum (pepper), seeded and cut into 8
1 red onion, peeled and quartered
85 g (3 oz/½ cup) pitted green Sicilian olives
6 kale leaves, white stems removed, torn into pieces
250 g (9 oz) small cherry tomatoes
1 tablespoon apple cider vinegar
2 tablespoons avocado oil

Chop the parsley for **5 sec/speed 5**. Scrape down the side of the bowl.

Add the capsicum, onion and olives. Chop for **5 sec/speed 5**. Scrape down the side of the bowl.

Add the kale, tomatoes, vinegar and oil. Mix for **10 sec/speed 2** then serve.

DAIRY-FREE | GLUTEN-FREE | NUT-FREE | VEGAN | VEGETARIAN

BABY POTATO AND EDAMAME SALAD

There is something about edamame that has my children addicted to eating them. They are also the perfect partner to potatoes in this super-fresh salad.

SERVES 4

Preparation time 10 minutes
Cooking time 30 minutes + cooling

60 ml (2 fl oz/¼ cup) avocado oil
2 tablespoons apple cider vinegar
1 tablespoon raw honey
1 tablespoon brown mustard seeds
600 g (1 lb 5 oz) baby potatoes (white- and red-skinned varieties), halved
185 g (6½ oz/1 cup) shelled edamame (soy beans)
2 baby cos (romaine) lettuces, trimmed and thickly sliced crossways into rounds
2 tablespoons chopped chives
2 tablespoons shelled pistachio nuts, chopped

Blend the oil, vinegar, honey and mustard seeds for **20 sec/speed 9**. Transfer the dressing mixture to a large heatproof bowl.

Add 500 ml (17 fl oz/2 cups) water to the mixer bowl. Attach the steaming bowl, instead of the measuring cup, to the mixer bowl lid. Add the potato and attach the steaming bowl lid. Cook for **25 min/steam mode/speed 1**. Add the edamame and cook for a further 5 minutes.

Transfer the vegetables to the bowl with the dressing mixture, tossing gently to coat. Leave to cool to room temperature.

Add all the remaining ingredients, toss gently to combine then serve.

DAIRY-FREE | GLUTEN-FREE | VEGAN | VEGETARIAN

RED SALAD WITH TAHINI MISO DRESSING

I just love any salad that has the power to stand on its own as a dish as well as being served as a side, like this one. I love the tahini and turmeric dressing – it makes this salad so moreish and satisfying.

SERVES 4

Preparation time 15 minutes

400 g (14 oz) beetroot (beets), skin scrubbed,
  cut into 8 wedges
1 bunch radishes, trimmed
300 g (10½ oz) red cabbage, cut into 3
1 tablespoon white miso paste
2 tablespoons unhulled tahini
finely grated zest and juice of 2 limes
80 ml (2½ fl oz/⅓ cup) warm tap water
1 spring onion (scallion), thinly sliced
2 teaspoons toasted sesame seeds

Chop the beetroot for **20 sec/speed 5**. Transfer to a bowl.

Chop the radishes for **5 sec/speed 5**. Transfer to the bowl with the beetroot.

Chop the cabbage for **5 sec/speed 5**. Add to the bowl with the beetroot and radish. Toss gently to combine. Set aside.

Mix the miso paste, tahini, lime zest and juice and the warm water for **10 sec/speed 4**.

Drizzle the dressing over the vegetables in the bowl. Sprinkle with the spring onion and toasted sesame seeds and serve.

DAIRY-FREE | GLUTEN-FREE | NUT-FREE | VEGAN | VEGETARIAN

VIETNAMESE SALAD

Yum – another super-tasty salad that is equally delicious served on its own as a hero lunch or alongside any of my Asian-style main recipes.

SERVES 4

Preparation time 10 minutes
Cooking time 2 minutes

1 long red chilli, halved and seeded
1 garlic clove
1 lemongrass stem, white part only, cut into
   3 cm (1¼ inch) lengths, bruised
2 tablespoons lime juice
2 tablespoons apple cider vinegar
1 tablespoon raw honey
300 g (10½ oz) Chinese cabbage (wong bok),
   cut into 4 cm (1½ inch) pieces
2 carrots, peeled into long thin strips with a vegetable peeler
2 Lebanese (short) cucumbers, peeled into long thin strips
   with a vegetable peeler
115 g (4 oz/1 cup) bean sprouts
1 large handful mint leaves

Chop the chilli, garlic and lemongrass for **5 sec/speed 7**. Scrape down the side of the bowl.

Add 60 ml (2 fl oz/¼ cup) water and cook for **2 min/120°C/speed 1**.

Transfer the mixture to a heatproof bowl. Stir through the lime juice, vinegar and honey until the honey dissolves. Set aside.

Chop the cabbage for **5 sec/speed 5**. Transfer to a large bowl. Add all the remaining ingredients and toss gently to combine. Spoon over the chilli mixture and serve.

DAIRY-FREE | GLUTEN-FREE | NUT-FREE | PALEO |
VEGETARIAN

QUICK PICKLED VEGIES

I can happily eat these straight from the container, but they are super-yummo served with Beef and lamb kofta (page 117) or Fish and vegie patties (page 129).

SERVES 4

Preparation time 10 minutes
Cooking time 3 minutes + cooling

4 baby fennel bulbs, trimmed and very thinly sliced
1 small red onion, very thinly sliced into rounds
1 bunch red radishes, very thinly sliced into rounds
250 ml (9 fl oz/1 cup) apple cider vinegar
2 tablespoons raw honey
1 tablespoon brown mustard seeds
2 teaspoons fennel seeds
1 small handful dill fronds

Place the fennel bulb, onion and radish in a large, flat heatproof dish and set aside.

Cook the vinegar, honey, mustard and fennel seeds for **3 min/120°C/ speed 1**.

Pour the hot vinegar mixture over the vegetables in the dish, turning to coat. Leave to cool to room temperature, turning occasionally.

Add the dill and toss to combine. Serve immediately or chill in an airtight container for up to 5 days.

DAIRY-FREE | GLUTEN-FREE | NUT-FREE | PALEO | VEGETARIAN

KOREAN STEAMED EGGPLANT

I never thought that eggplant could be cooked and served so simply, yet have so much flavour. This is simply divine with Korean beef (page 116).

SERVES 4

Preparation time 5 minutes
Cooking time 5 minutes + standing

3 garlic cloves
3 spring onions (scallions)
½ teaspoon dried chilli flakes
1 tablespoon sesame seeds
1 tablespoon sesame oil
60 ml (2 fl oz/¼ cup) tamari (gluten-free soy sauce)
8 baby finger (long thin) eggplants (aubergines), trimmed,
    halved lengthways and cut diagonally into 3 cm (1¼ inch) lengths

Chop the garlic and spring onions for **5 sec/speed 7**. Scrape down the side of the bowl.

Add the chilli flakes, sesame seeds, oil and tamari. Mix for **5 sec/speed 5**.

Transfer the garlic mixture to a large heatproof bowl and set aside.

Add 500 ml (17 fl oz/2 cups) water to the mixer bowl. Attach the steaming bowl, instead of the measuring cup, to the mixer bowl lid. Add the eggplant. Attach the steaming bowl lid. Cook for **5 min/steam mode/speed 1**.

Transfer the eggplant to a bowl with the garlic mixture and toss well to coat. Leave to stand for 5 minutes, tossing occasionally. Serve warm.

DAIRY-FREE | GLUTEN-FREE | NUT-FREE | PALEO | VEGAN |
VEGETARIAN

STEAMED ASIAN GREENS

This has all the taste of yum cha, but with no fuss. I will often have these greens just as they are, served over some brown rice – a great meal for one when the rest of the family is out.

SERVES 4

Preparation time 5 minutes
Cooking time 5 minutes

1 garlic clove
3 cm (1¼ inch) piece fresh ginger, peeled and halved
2 spring onions (scallions), cut into 5 cm (2 inch) pieces
1 tablespoon Stock 'cube' of choice (pages 34–5)
2 teaspoons tamari (gluten-free soy sauce)
1 bunch Chinese broccoli (gai larn), halved crossways
1 bunch baby bok choy (pak choy), halved lengthways
1 handful coriander (cilantro) leaves, to serve

Chop the garlic, ginger and spring onion for **10 sec/speed 7**. Scrape down the side of the bowl. Add the stock cube, tamari and 125 ml (4 fl oz/½ cup) water.

Attach the steaming bowl, instead of the measuring cup, to the mixer bowl lid. Add the Chinese broccoli and then top with the bok choy. Attach the steaming bowl lid. Cook for **5 min/steam mode/speed 1**.

Transfer the vegetables to a flat serving bowl. Spoon over the stock mixture from the mixer bowl. Top with the coriander and serve hot.

DAIRY-FREE | GLUTEN-FREE | NUT-FREE | PALEO | VEGAN | VEGETARIAN

BROCCOLI AND CASHEW TABOULEH

Raw, crunchy and packed with zing, this tabouleh is my go-to gluten-free side that is great served with Beef and lamb kofta (page 117) or Falafel patties (page 136).

SERVES 4

Preparation time 10 minutes

155 g (5½ oz/1 cup) raw cashew nuts
1 garlic clove
1 large handful basil leaves
1 large handful mint leaves
1 bunch flat-leaf (Italian) parsley, torn in half
2 teaspoons sumac
1 teaspoon sea salt
finely grated zest and juice of 1 small lemon
2 tablespoons macadamia oil
600 g (1 lb 5 oz) broccoli, stems removed
lemon wedges, to serve

Chop the cashew nuts, garlic, basil, mint and parsley for **5 sec/speed 7**. Scrape down the side of the bowl.

Add all the remaining ingredients and chop for **5 sec/speed 5**. Serve with the lemon wedges.

DAIRY-FREE | GLUTEN-FREE | PALEO | VEGAN | VEGETARIAN

CORIANDER BLACK BEANS WITH AVOCADO

Kidney bean chilli (page 141) and this side dish are the best of friends – there's no need to be scared of a double dose of beans. Pop these inside the Spinach and corn tortillas (page 68) and wrap up for a great lunch.

SERVES 4

Preparation time 5 minutes + standing

1 small handful coriander (cilantro), torn in half
1 long red chilli, halved and seeded
1 garlic clove
finely grated zest and juice of 2 limes
60 ml (2 fl oz/¼ cup) avocado oil
1 teaspoon cumin seeds
400 g (14 oz/2 cups) cooked black beans (see page 37)
1 avocado, thinly sliced

Chop the coriander, chilli and garlic for **5 sec/speed 7**. Scrape down the side of the bowl.

Add the lime zest and juice, oil and cumin seeds. Mix for **10 sec/speed 7**. Transfer the dressing to a large bowl.

Add the black beans to the dressing in the bowl, tossing to combine. Leave to stand for 20 minutes to macerate.

Add the avocado, gently turning to combine, then serve.

DAIRY-FREE | GLUTEN-FREE | NUT-FREE | VEGAN | VEGETARIAN

ALMOND BROWN BASMATI PILAF

Fluffy, delicious rice cooked to perfection — enough said!

SERVES 4

Preparation time 5 minutes
Cooking time 40 minutes

80 g (2¾ oz/½ cup) whole natural almonds
2 spring onions (scallions), cut into 4 cm (1½ inch) lengths
400 g (14 oz) brown basmati rice, very well rinsed
2 tablespoons Stock 'cube' of choice (pages 34–5)
50 g (1¾ oz) butter, chopped

Chop the almonds and spring onion for **5 sec/speed 7**. Transfer the mixture to a bowl and set aside.

Add 900 ml (31 fl oz) water to the mixer bowl. Place the rice in the simmering basket. Insert the rice-filled simmering basket into the mixer bowl. Add the stock cube and butter and cook for **20 min/100°C/ speed 4**. Add 500 ml (17 fl oz/2 cups) extra water to the mixer bowl. Cook for **20 min/100°C/speed 4**.

Remove the simmering basket insert from the mixer bowl and drain the rice well.

Transfer the drained rice to a heatproof bowl. Add the almond mixture and toss gently to combine. Serve hot.

GLUTEN-FREE | VEGETARIAN

WILD RICE AND PINEAPPLE SALAD

This screams summer to me every time I make it. If you keep the fresh leaves separate, you can make this the day before for an even better flavour.

SERVES 4

Preparation time 10 minutes
Cooking time 1 hour + cooling

1 red onion, peeled and quartered
200 g (7 oz) pineapple, peeled, cored and cut into
    5 cm (2 inch) pieces
2 tablespoons apple cider vinegar
2 tablespoons avocado oil
2 tablespoons Stock 'cube' of choice (pages 34–5)
200 g (7 oz) wild rice, very well rinsed
2 zucchini (courgettes), halved lengthways,
    diagonally sliced into 3 cm (1¼ inch) lengths
1 large handful watercress leaves
25 g (1 oz) baby rocket (arugula) leaves
1 small handful mint leaves

Chop the onion for **5 sec/speed 5**. Scrape down the side of the bowl.

Add the pineapple and chop for **3 sec/speed 5**. Scrape down the side of the bowl.

Add the vinegar and oil. Mix for **10 sec/reverse stir/speed 4**. Transfer the pineapple mixture to a large heatproof bowl.

Add 1 litre (35 fl oz/4 cups) water and the stock cubes to the mixer bowl. Place the rice in the simmering basket. Insert the rice-filled simmering basket into the mixer bowl.

Attach the steaming bowl, instead of the measuring cup, to the mixer bowl lid. Cook for **60 min/steam mode/speed 4**, adding the zucchini to the steaming bowl in the last 10 minutes of cooking.

Attach the steaming bowl lid.

Transfer the zucchini to the bowl with the pineapple mixture.

Remove the simmering basket insert from the mixer bowl. Drain the rice well and add it to the pineapple mixture, tossing gently to combine. Leave to cool to room temperature.

Add all the remaining ingredients, tossing gently to combine, then serve.

DAIRY-FREE |
GLUTEN-FREE
| NUT-FREE
| VEGAN |
VEGETARIAN

RAW RAINBOW VEGETABLE 'RICE'

This rainbow rice is a great alternative to your standard fried rice side dish and an absolute winner for getting some extra vegies packed into your family's meals. They will love the colour, texture and sweet flavour of this dish.

SERVES 4
Preparation time 5 minutes
Cooking time 3 minutes

400 g (14 oz) cauliflower florets
400 g (14 oz) broccoli florets
1 carrot, cut into 3
1 zucchini (courgette), cut into 3
1 beetroot (beet), peeled and cut into thick wedges
2 garlic cloves
4 cm (1½ inch) piece fresh ginger, peeled
2 tablespoons Garlic frying oil (page 21)
2 teaspoons sesame oil
2 tablespoons tamari (gluten-free soy sauce)
1 tablespoon toasted sesame seeds (see Note)

Chop the cauliflower for **2 sec/speed 5**. Scrape down the side of the bowl. Chop again for **2 sec/speed 5**. Transfer to a large bowl. Chop the broccoli for **2 sec/speed 5**. Scrape down the side of the bowl. Chop again for **2 sec/speed 5**. Add to the bowl with the cauliflower.

Chop the carrot and zucchini for **2 sec/speed 5**. Scrape down the side of the bowl. Chop again for **2 sec/speed 5**. Transfer to the bowl with the cauliflower and broccoli.

Chop the beetroot for **2 sec/speed 5**. Scrape down the side of the bowl. Chop again for **2 sec/speed 5**. Transfer the beetroot to the bowl with the other vegetables.

Chop the garlic and ginger for **5 sec/speed 7**. Scrape down the side of the bowl.

Add both oils and the tamari. Cook for **3 min/100°C/speed 1**. Add this mixture to the vegetables in the bowl, tossing well to combine. Top with the sesame seeds and serve.

DAIRY-FREE | GLUTEN-FREE | NUT-FREE | PALEO | VEGAN | VEGETARIAN

NOTE
I purchase ready-toasted sesame seeds from Asian grocers.

TOMATO-BRAISED GREEN BEANS

These guys are lovely served alongside the Meatballs in mustard sauce (page 106), Fish and vege patties (page 129) or even just with scrambled eggs at breakfast.

SERVES 4
Preparation time 5 minutes
Cooking time 8 minutes

300 g (10½ oz) green beans, trimmed and cut into 5 cm (2 inch) lengths
2 tablespoons Stock 'cube' of choice (pages 34–5)
60 g (2¼ oz/½ cup) Tomato mix (page 28)
1 small handful flat-leaf (Italian) parsley leaves

Cook the beans, stock cube, tomato mix and 60 ml (2 fl oz/¼ cup) water for **8 min/100°C/reverse stir/speed 1**.

Add the parsley and mix for **30 sec/reverse stir/speed 1**. Serve the beans hot.

DAIRY-FREE | GLUTEN-FREE | NUT-FREE | VEGAN | VEGETARIAN

CAULIFLOWER AND SWEET POTATO SMASH

I'm totally addicted to all forms of hot, buttery smashed vegetables. The combo of sweet potato and cauliflower is my hands-down favourite at the moment and just must be served with Chunky beef pie (page 114).

SERVES 4

Preparation time 5 minutes
Cooking time 23 minutes

500 g (1 lb 2 oz) sweet potatoes, skin scrubbed,
    cut into 2 cm (¾ inch) pieces
400 g (14 oz) cauliflower florets
4 spring onions (scallions), cut into 4 cm (1½ inch) lengths
1 garlic clove
50 g (1¾ oz) butter
60 ml (2 fl oz/¼ cup) cream of choice (cow's or coconut)

Add 500 ml (17 fl oz/2 cups) water to the mixer bowl. Attach the steaming bowl, instead of the measuring cup, to the mixer bowl lid. Add the potato, then the cauliflower. Attach the steaming bowl lid. Cook for **20 min/steam mode/speed 1**.

Transfer the vegetables to a heatproof bowl. Discard the water from the mixer bowl.

Chop the spring onion and garlic for **5 sec/speed 7**. Scrape down the side of the bowl.

Add the butter and cream. Cook for **3 min/100°C/speed 1**.

Transfer the cream mixture to the bowl with the vegetables. Mash them together lightly. Serve hot.

GLUTEN-FREE | NUT-FREE | VEGETARIAN

CAULIFLOWER FOCACCIA

No kneading, no yeast and yet super-filling and moreish –
just like your standard focaccia. This is the perfect dipping
accompaniment to the recipes in the soups chapter, or served
alongside your favourite lunchtime salad – or even scrambled
eggs at brekkie.

SERVES 6

Preparation time 5 minutes
Cooking time 30 minutes

100 g (3½ oz) whole natural almonds
50 g (1¾ oz/¼ cup) tapioca pearls
600 g (1 lb 5 oz) small cauliflower florets
3 eggs
2 tablespoons rosemary leaves
2 tablespoons Garlic frying oil (page 21), softened
2 teaspoons sea salt

Preheat the oven to 200°C (400°F)/180°C (350°F) fan-forced.
Line a large baking tray with baking paper.

Mill the almonds and tapioca for **30 sec/speed 9**. Scrape down the
side of the bowl. Add the cauliflower and chop for **5 sec/speed 7**.
Scrape down the side of the bowl. Chop again for **3 sec/speed 7**.

Add the eggs and mix for **30 sec/speed 5**.

Transfer the mixture to the prepared tray. Flatten out the mixture
to a rectangle about 2 cm (¾ inch) thick.

Using your fingertips, make indents all over the surface. Top with
the rosemary, garlic frying oil and salt. Bake for 30 minutes or until
cooked and golden. Serve hot.

DAIRY-FREE | GLUTEN-FREE | PALEO | VEGETARIAN

SWEET CHILLI CARROTS

Serve these carrots with Chunky beef pie (page 114) or Meatballs in mustard sauce (page 106).

SERVES 4

Preparation time 5 minutes
Cooking time 9 minutes

1 long red chilli, halved and seeded
2 garlic cloves
2 cm (¾ inch) piece fresh ginger, peeled
2 cm (¾ inch) piece fresh turmeric or 1 teaspoon ground turmeric
1 tablespoon pure maple syrup
2 tablespoons lemon juice
50 g (1¾ oz) butter
2 bunches baby carrots, trimmed, skins scrubbed

Chop the chilli, garlic, ginger and turmeric for **5 sec/speed 7**. Scrape down the side of the bowl. Add the maple syrup, lemon juice and butter. Cook for **3 min/100°C/speed 1**.

Transfer the mixture to a heatproof bowl. Cover to keep warm and set aside.

Place 500 ml (17 fl oz/2 cups) water in the mixer bowl. Attach the steaming bowl, instead of the measuring cup, to the mixer bowl lid. Add the carrots. Attach the steaming bowl lid. Cook for **6 min/steam mode/speed 1**.

Transfer the carrots to a serving plate. Add the butter mixture and toss to coat. Serve hot.

See photograph on pages 168–9.

GLUTEN-FREE | NUT-FREE | VEGETARIAN

SIMPLE BUTTERY VEG

I could literally just eat a bowl of this for dinner on its own, with a sprinkling of sea salt and a splash of lemon juice. Honestly, if you serve this with most of the main recipes in this book, you won't be disappointed.

SERVES 4

Preparation time 5 minutes
Cooking time 12 minutes

1 handful flat-leaf (Italian) parsley leaves
80 g (2¾ oz) butter, at room temperature
1 tablespoon Stock 'cube' of choice (pages 34–5)
1 corn cob, cut into 8 crossways
300 g (10½ oz) broccoli florets
200 g (7 oz) green beans, trimmed

Chop the parsley for **3 sec/speed 7**. Scrape down the side of the bowl.

Add the butter and stock cube. Mix for **10 sec/speed 5**. Transfer the butter mixture to a large heatproof bowl.

Add 500 ml (17 fl oz/2 cups) water to the mixer bowl. Attach the steaming bowl, instead of the measuring cup, to the mixer bowl lid. Add the corn, then the broccoli and beans. Attach the steaming bowl lid. Cook for **12 min/steam mode/speed 1**.

Transfer the vegetables to the bowl with the butter mixture. Toss gently to coat and serve hot.

See photograph on pages 168–9.

GLUTEN-FREE | NUT-FREE | VEGETARIAN

SIMPLE
BUTTERY VEG
(PAGE 166)

SWEET
CHILLI
CARROTS
(PAGE 166)

MUSHY PEAS

Chunky beef pie (page 114) and these peas are the best of friends. One should never, ever be served without the other – absolutely yum!

SERVES 4

Preparation time 5 minutes + soaking
Cooking time 25 minutes

220 g (7¾ oz/1 cup) dried green split peas, soaked overnight, drained
2 tablespoons Stock 'cube' of choice (pages 34–5)
140 g (5 oz/1 cup) frozen peas

Add the split peas, 750 ml (26 fl oz/3 cups) water and the stock cube to the mixer bowl. Attach the simmering basket, instead of the measuring cup, to the mixer bowl lid. Cook for **20 min/100°C/speed 1**.

Add the frozen peas through the hole in the mixer bowl lid. Cook for **5 min/120°C/speed 1**. Serve the peas hot.

DAIRY-FREE | GLUTEN-FREE | NUT-FREE | VEGAN | VEGETARIAN

BEAN, CELERIAC AND THYME PURÉE

This purée was a favourite for both my children when they first started eating solid food. It's now one of our staple sides in place of standard mashed potatoes.

SERVES 4

Preparation time 10 minutes
Cooking time 15 minutes

450 g (1 lb) celeriac, peeled and cut into 3 cm (1¼ inch) pieces
50 g (1¾ oz) butter
1 tablespoon Stock 'cube' of choice (pages 34–5)
2 teaspoons thyme leaves
200 g (7 oz/1 cup) cooked red kidney beans (page 37)
125 ml (4 fl oz/½ cup) thin (pouring/whipping) cream

Chop the celeriac for **10 sec/speed 6**. Scrape down the side of the bowl.

Add the butter, stock cube and 80 ml (2½ fl oz/⅓ cup) water. Cook for **10 min/100°C/speed 1**.

Add the thyme, beans and cream. Cook for **5 min/100°C/speed 1**.

Blend for **30 sec/speed 8** then serve.

GLUTEN-FREE | NUT-FREE | VEGETARIAN

FRENCH-DRESSED LENTILS

So deliciously fresh tasting, these little lentils are the best side to serve with Beef bourguignon (page 108).

SERVES 4
Preparation time 5 minutes
Cooking time 5 minutes

1 carrot, cut into 3
2 celery stalks, cut into 4 cm (1½ inch) lengths
2 spring onions (scallions), cut into 4 cm (1½ inch) lengths
3 tablespoons French tarragon leaves
50 g (1¾ oz) butter, chopped
1 teaspoon sea salt
¼ teaspoon ground white pepper
2 teaspoons thyme leaves
finely grated zest and juice of 2 lemons
300 g (10½ oz) cooked French blue-green lentils (page 37)
1 handful flat-leaf (Italian) parsley leaves

Chop the carrot, celery, spring onion and tarragon for **5 sec/speed 7**. Scrape down the side of the bowl.

Add the butter, salt, pepper and thyme. Cook for **5 min/120°C/speed 1**. Transfer the vegetable mixture to a large heatproof bowl.

Add the lemon zest and juice, lentils and parsley to the vegetable mixture in the bowl, tossing gently to combine. Serve warm.

GLUTEN-FREE | NUT-FREE | VEGETARIAN

BRAISED LEEK AND CELERY

The celery in this braise becomes very sweet after cooking so you will soon learn that one dollop alongside your main meal will never be enough!

SERVES 4

Preparation time 10 minutes
Cooking time 12 minutes

2 garlic cloves
4 celery stalks, trimmed and cut into 4 cm (1½ inch) lengths
2 leeks, white part only, thinly sliced into rounds
50 g (1¾ oz) butter
1 teaspoon celery seeds
125 ml (4 fl oz/½ cup) Golden chicken broth (page 74)
1 large handful flat-leaf (Italian) parsley leaves

Chop the garlic and celery for **5 sec/speed 7**. Scrape down the side of the bowl.

Add the leek, butter, celery seeds and broth. Cook for **12 min/90°C/ reverse stir/speed 1**.

Add the parsley, stir for **20 sec/reverse stir/speed 2**, then serve.

GLUTEN-FREE | NUT-FREE

FENNEL REMOULADE

This creamy little side is so crunchy and refreshing. Enjoy it with grilled fish or a beef roast. It's quite lovely over slices of toasted Melt 'n' mix bread (page 56), too.

SERVES 4

Preparation time 10 minutes

80 g (2¾ oz/½ cup) whole natural almonds
3 tablespoons French tarragon leaves
2 large handfuls flat-leaf (Italian) parsley leaves
6 baby fennel bulbs, trimmed and cut into 3
4 celery stalks, trimmed and cut into 4 cm (1½ inch) lengths
1 small lemon, peel and white pith removed, quartered, seeds removed
1 small garlic clove
3 cm (1¼ inch) piece fresh turmeric, peeled
185 g (6½ oz/¾ cup) Avo mayo (page 26)

Chop the almonds, tarragon and parsley for **3 sec/speed 7**. Scrape down the side of the bowl.

Add the fennel and celery. Chop for **3 sec/speed 7**. Transfer the mixture to a large bowl. Set aside.

Add the lemon flesh, garlic and turmeric. Chop for **5 sec/speed 7**. Scrape down the side of the bowl.

Add the avo mayo and mix for **10 sec/speed 4**. Transfer the mayo mixture to the bowl with the fennel mixture. Stir until well combined. Serve immediately or chill for up to 1 day in an airtight container.

DAIRY-FREE | GLUTEN-FREE | PALEO | VEGETARIAN

wholesome
sweets

VEGAN STRAWBERRY 'CHEESECAKE'

I have fooled many people by presenting this as a standard cheesecake. The texture from the blended cashew nuts is what turns this vegan-friendly dessert into a moreish and creamy alternative to the standard.

SERVES 8

Preparation time 10 minutes + soaking + freezing

200 g (7 oz/2 cups) pecans, plus extra chopped pecans for garnish
6 medjool dates, pitted and halved
310 g (11 oz/2 cups) raw cashew nuts, soaked overnight, drained and rinsed
125 ml (4 fl oz/½ cup) coconut oil
finely grated zest and juice of 1 small lemon
80 ml (2½ fl oz/⅓ cup) pure maple syrup
250 g (9 oz) ripe strawberries, hulled, plus extra half strawberries for garnish

Line the base and sides of a 20 cm (8 inch) square cake tin with baking paper.

Blend the pecans, dates and 1 tablespoon water for **30 sec/speed 7**. Transfer the pecan mixture to the prepared tin, pressing down firmly to cover the base.

Blend the cashew nuts, oil, lemon zest and juice, maple syrup and strawberries for **1 min/speed 9**.

Pour the strawberry mixture over the pecan mixture in the base of the tin. Freeze for 3 hours or until almost set firm.

Transfer the 'cheesecake' to a board and cut it into eight pieces. Serve chilled. Garnish with the extra strawberry halves and the chopped pecans.

DAIRY-FREE | GLUTEN-FREE | PALEO | VEGAN | VEGETARIAN

PASSIONFRUIT PUDDINGS

These puddings are almost panna cotta-like – but with absolutely no fuss. Plus, they're packed full of the health benefits that chia seeds have to offer.

SERVES 4

Preparation time 5 minutes + standing + chilling

120 g (4¼ oz/⅔ cup) chia seeds
500 ml (17 fl oz/2 cups) Vanilla pepita milk (page 16)
1 tablespoon raw honey
4 passionfruit, halved, seeds scraped

Mix the chia seeds, vanilla pepita milk and honey for **10 sec/speed 5**. Scrape down the side of the bowl. Leave to stand for 5 minutes.

Mix again for **10 sec/speed 5**.

Blend for **1 min/speed 9**. Divide the chia mixture evenly among four glasses. Top with the passionfruit pulp and chill for 1 hour. Serve immediately or cover and chill for up to 3 days.

DAIRY-FREE | GLUTEN-FREE | NUT-FREE | PALEO |
VEGETARIAN

LEMON DELICIOUS

This is one of those heart-warming, show-stopper desserts, which needs a super-quick delivery to the table straight from the oven. Be sure to have everyone seated and ready to witness, or get them in the kitchen to see the magical high-rise top of zesty deliciousness emerge from the oven – then listen to the oooohs and ahhhhs.

SERVES 6

Preparation time 10 minutes
Cooking time 50 minutes

60 g (2¼ oz) butter, at room temperature
2 tablespoons whole wheat grains (see Note page 45)
1 tablespoon tapioca pearls
3 eggs, separated
80 ml (2½ fl oz/⅓ cup) raw honey
1 teaspoon baking powder
185 ml (6 fl oz/¾ cup) milk of choice
80 ml (2½ fl oz/⅓ cup) lemon juice

Preheat the oven to 180°C (350°F)/160°C (315°F) fan-forced. Use a little of the butter to grease the base and side of a deep 1 litre (35 fl oz/4 cup capacity) oval baking dish. Set the dish inside a large, deep baking tin.

Mill the wheat grains and tapioca for **1 min/speed 10**. Transfer the mixture to a bowl. Wash and thoroughly dry the mixer bowl.

Insert the whisk attachment into the clean, dry mixer bowl. Add the egg whites and whisk for **2 min/speed 3**.

Transfer the softly beaten egg whites to a bowl and set aside.

Add the yolks, honey and butter to the mixer and whisk for **2 min/speed 3**. Scrape down the side of the bowl.

Add the baking powder, milk, lemon juice and reserved milled wheat mixture. Whisk for **30 sec/speed 7**. Scrape down the side of the bowl.

Return the reserved softly beaten egg whites to the mixture in the mixer bowl. Whisk for **3 sec/speed 3**.

Transfer the lemon mixture to the prepared dish, levelling the surface. Fill the large baking tin with boiling water until it reaches halfway up the side of the dish with the lemon mixture. Bake for 45–50 minutes or until puffed and golden. Serve immediately, straight from the oven.

NUT-FREE |
VEGETARIAN

LITTLE CITRUS MACADAMIA CAKES

There is so much citrus love in these super-moist muffins. My mum just swoons over these little morsels. They are perfect on their own with a hot cuppa, but I cannot lie – they're also delicious with a drizzle of thin (pouring/whipping) cream or a dollop of Cow's milk yoghurt (page 14).

MAKES 12

Preparation time 15 minutes
Cooking time 1 hour 10 minutes + cooling

210 g (7½ oz) raw macadamia nuts, plus extra to decorate
1 orange
1 lime
125 ml (4 fl oz/½ cup) raw honey
3 eggs
1 teaspoon baking powder
finely grated lime zest, to serve

Mill the macadamia nuts for **3 sec/speed 9**. Transfer to a bowl and set aside.

Pour 1 litre (35 fl oz/4 cups) water into the mixer bowl. Insert the simmering basket. Place the orange and lime in the simmering basket. Cook for **45 min/steam mode/speed 2**. Carefully transfer the citrus to a heatproof board. Leave to cool. Clean the mixer bowl.

Preheat the oven to 180°C (350°F)/160°C (315°F) fan-forced. Line a 12-hole, 80 ml (2½ fl oz/⅓ cup) capacity muffin tin with paper cases.

Remove the top and bottom (about 3 mm/⅛ inch) from the orange and lime and discard. Quarter the orange and lime and remove and discard any seeds. Place the citrus flesh into the cleaned mixer bowl. Add the honey, eggs, baking powder and reserved milled macadamia nuts to the citrus flesh in the mixer bowl. Mix for **10 sec/speed 7**.
Scrape down the side of the bowl. Mix again for **10 sec/speed 7**.

Divide the citrus mixture evenly among the paper cases in the muffin tin. Top with the extra macadamia nuts.

Bake for 25 minutes or until cooked and golden. Leave to cool in the tin for 20 minutes. Serve warm or at room temperature, sprinkled with lime zest. Keep in an airtight container for up to 3 days.

DAIRY-FREE |
GLUTEN-FREE
| PALEO |
VEGETARIAN

CARAMEL FUDGE FINGERS

This is the closest you will ever get to a traditional fudge without the added nasties, refined sugar or kitchen labour.

MAKES 10 PIECES

Preparation time 10 minutes + freezing

100 g (3½ oz/1 cup) pepitas (pumpkin seeds)
115 g (4 oz) sunflower seeds
60 ml (2 fl oz/¼ cup) coconut oil, plus 125 ml (4 fl oz/½ cup) extra
180 g (6½ oz/⅔ cup) unhulled tahini
12 medjool dates, pitted and halved
80 ml (2½ fl oz/⅓ cup) Coconut cream (page 17)

Line the base and sides of a 10 x 20 cm (4 x 8 inch) loaf (bar) tin with baking paper.

Chop the pepitas and sunflower seeds for **10 sec/speed 5**. Scrape down the side of the bowl. Transfer half the seed mixture to a bowl and set aside.

Add the coconut oil to the remaining seed mixture in the mixer bowl. Mix for **5 sec/speed 5**.

Transfer the seed paste to the prepared loaf tin, pushing the mixture down firmly to evenly cover the base.

Blend the tahini, dates, coconut cream and extra coconut oil for **30 sec/ speed 9**. Pour this caramel mixture over the seed paste base in the prepared tin and level the surface.

Press the reserved seed mixture on top of the caramel mixture in the pan. Freeze for 20 minutes or until almost set firm.

Transfer the fudge to a board and cut it into 10 pieces crossways. Serve chilled.

DAIRY-FREE | GLUTEN-FREE | NUT-FREE | PALEO | VEGAN | VEGETARIAN

MINI RASPBERRY BROWNIES

I've never come across a person who doesn't enjoy a brownie. These babies can be made and chilled for up to 3 days ahead, so they're great for party table fare.

MAKES 12

Preparation time 5 minutes
Cooking time 22 minutes + cooling

155 g (5½ oz/1 cup) raw macadamia nuts
125 g (4½ oz) unsalted butter, chopped
70 g (2½ oz) carob powder
80 ml (2½ fl oz/⅓ cup) pure maple syrup
4 eggs
1 teaspoon pure vanilla
125 g (4½ oz) raspberries

Preheat the oven to 160°C (315°F)/140°C (275°F) fan-forced. Line a 12-hole, 80 ml (2½ fl oz/⅓ cup) capacity muffin tin with paper cases.

Mill the macadamia nuts for **10 sec/speed 9**. Transfer to a bowl.

Melt the butter for **2 min/120°C/speed 1**. Add the carob powder and maple syrup. Mix for **10 sec/speed 4**. Scrape down the side of the bowl.

Add the eggs, vanilla and reserved milled macadamia nuts. Mix for **20 sec/speed 5**.

Spoon the batter mixture evenly among the prepared paper cases in the tin. Top with the raspberries. Bake for 20 minutes or until cooked around the edges but still a little soft in the centres.

Leave to cool in the tin, then serve.

GLUTEN-FREE | VEGETARIAN

VANILLA COCONUT MARSHMALLOW

Marshmallow just got easy to make! Our children literally go crazy over these coconut gems. These make a perfect party treat, too – for all age groups.

MAKES 16

Preparation time 20 minutes
Cooking time 10 minutes + standing + chilling

45 g (1½ oz/¼ cup) tapioca pearls
50 g (1¾ oz) flaked coconut
3 vanilla beans, halved lengthways, seeds scraped
40 g (1½ oz/¼ cup) powdered gelatine
250 ml (9 fl oz/1 cup) raw honey

Line the base and sides of a 20 cm (8 inch) square cake tin with non-stick baking paper.

Mill the tapioca pearls for **30 sec/speed 10**. Scrape down the side of the bowl.

Add the coconut and half the vanilla seeds. Mill for **30 sec/speed 9**. Transfer the coconut mixture to a bowl.

Using half the coconut mixture, dust the base of the prepared tin. Set aside.

Insert the whisk attachment into the mixer bowl. Add 125 ml (4 fl oz/½ cup) water and the gelatine, making sure the gelatine doesn't touch the blade or the whisk. Mix for **30 sec/speed 2**. Leave to stand.

Combine the honey, remaining vanilla seeds and 125 ml (4 fl oz/½ cup) water in a small saucepan over high heat. Cook, swirling the pan occasionally, until the mixture starts to come to the boil.

Reduce the heat to medium–high and rapidly simmer, untouched, until the mixture reaches 130°C (266°F) on a confectionery thermometer (soft crack stage). Remove the pan from the heat and allow the bubbles to settle.

Slowly pour the hot honey mixture into the gelatine mixture in the mixer bowl, while whisking, for **1 min/speed 4**. Continue whisking for **15 min/speed 4**.

Working quickly, spoon the marshmallow into the prepared tin over the dust mixture. Level the surface. Sprinkle the top of the marshmallow evenly with the remaining coconut mixture. Leave to stand at room temperature for 6 hours or until set. Chill for 4 hours.

Transfer the marshmallow to a board. Using a large damp knife, cut the marshmallow into 16 pieces, then serve.

DAIRY-FREE |
GLUTEN-FREE |
NUT-FREE |
PALEO

LEMON PEPITA BALLS

These dried-fruit-free alternatives to a regular 'bliss ball' often feature in our fridge. I keep them in an airtight container, making them the perfect little sweet popper whenever you feel like one.

MAKES 16

Preparation time 10 minutes

100 g (3½ oz) flaked coconut
155 g (5½ oz/1 cup) pepitas (pumpkin seeds)
finely grated zest and juice of 1 small lemon
1 tablespoon psyllium husks
1 tablespoon unhulled tahini
1 tablespoon raw honey

Chop the coconut and pepitas for **5 sec/speed 9**. Scrape down the side of the bowl.

Transfer 4 tablespoons of the coconut mixture to a large plate and set aside.

Add the lemon zest and juice, psyllium husks, tahini and honey to the coconut in the mixer bowl. Blend for **5 sec/speed 7**. Scrape down the side of the bowl. Blend again for **10 sec/speed 5**.

Roll level tablespoon measures of the mixture into balls. Roll the balls lightly in the reserved coconut mixture. Serve immediately or chill in an airtight container for up to 1 week.

DAIRY-FREE | GLUTEN-FREE | NUT-FREE | PALEO | VEGETARIAN

RICOTTA CHEESECAKE

The simplicity of this cheesecake is what always wins people over. It's so deliciously light, yet creamy, and the subtle lemon flavour makes it a crowd pleaser. It's also a great make-ahead recipe, as you can keep it in an airtight container for up to 3 days.

SERVES 8

Preparation 10 minutes + soaking + chilling

310 g (11 oz/2 cups) raw macadamia nuts
8 medjool dates, seeded and halved
1 teaspoon mixed (pumpkin pie) spice
310 g (11 oz/2 cups) raw cashew nuts, soaked overnight, drained and rinsed
185 ml (6 fl oz/¾ cup) coconut oil
finely grated zest and juice of 1 lemon
460 g (1 lb/2 cups) Fresh ricotta (page 12)
1 teaspoon pure vanilla
80 ml (2½ fl oz/⅓ cup) raw honey
freshly grated nutmeg, to serve

Line the base and side of a 20 cm (8 inch) round spring-form cake tin with non-stick baking paper.

Blend the macadamia nuts, dates, mixed spice and 1 tablespoon water for **20 sec/speed 7**.

Transfer the macadamia mixture to the prepared tin, pressing the mixture down firmly to cover the base.

Blend the cashew nuts, oil, lemon zest and juice, ricotta, vanilla and honey for **1 min/speed 9**.

Pour the ricotta mixture over the macadamia mixture in the base of the tin. Chill for 4 hours or until set firm.

Transfer the cheesecake to a board, carefully release the side of the tin and cut the cheesecake into 8 slices. Top with freshly grated nutmeg. Serve chilled.

GLUTEN-FREE | VEGETARIAN

CREAMED RICE WITH SPICED SYRUP

It goes without saying that a warm bowl of creamed rice is delicious. However, the beauty of this recipe is that if there happen to be any leftovers, you can spoon them into serving glasses and chill for up to 3 days for another night's sweet treat.

SERVES 4

Preparation time 10 minutes
Cooking time 63 minutes

125 ml (4 fl oz/½ cup) pure maple syrup,
    plus 1 tablespoon extra
2 tablespoons lemon juice
2 star anise
1 cinnamon stick
3 cm (1¼ inch) piece fresh ginger, peeled and sliced
250 ml (9 fl oz/1 cup) milk of choice
410 ml (14 fl oz) Coconut milk (page 17)
165 g (5¾ oz/¾ cup) medium-grain brown rice, rinsed
½ teaspoon pure vanilla
fresh figs, to serve
freshly grated nutmeg, to serve

Cook the maple syrup, lemon juice, star anise, cinnamon and ginger for **3 min/120°C/speed 1**. Transfer the syrup mixture to a heatproof bowl and set aside.

Cook the milk, coconut milk, extra maple syrup, 125 ml (4 fl oz/½ cup) water, the rice and vanilla for **1 hour/100°C/reverse stir/speed 1**.

Divide the mixture among four serving bowls. Strain the cooled reserved spiced syrup and spoon over the rice. Top with the fresh figs and nutmeg and serve hot.

GLUTEN-FREE | NUT-FREE | VEGETARIAN

MEXICAN CHOCOLATE POTS

OK, this is adults-only fare – a treat that you will find in my fridge if we have people over for a special event.

SERVES 6

Preparation time 10 minutes
Cooking time 4 minutes + chilling

600 ml (21 fl oz) thin (pouring/whipping) cream
250 ml (9 fl oz/1 cup) cow's milk
450 g (1 lb) dark chocolate (70% cocoa solids), broken into pieces
1 teaspoon ground cinnamon
¼ teaspoon ground chilli
75 g (2¾ oz/½ cup) shelled pistachio nuts, chopped
lime wedges, to serve

Insert the whisk attachment into the mixer bowl. Add the cream and whisk for **20 sec/speed 4**. Transfer the softly whipped cream to a bowl and set aside.

Cook the milk, chocolate, cinnamon and chilli for **2 min/60°C/speed 4**. Scrape down the side of the bowl. Cook again for **2 min/60°C/speed 4**.

Return the softly whipped cream to the mixer bowl with the chocolate mixture. Mix for **30 sec/speed 1**.

Divide the chocolate cream among six glasses. Chill for 4 hours.

Top with the chopped pistachio nuts and serve with the lime wedges.

GLUTEN-FREE | VEGETARIAN

BLUEBERRY COCONUT 'CHOCOLATES'

Here's a great gift idea for the holiday season or for birthdays. It's so adaptable as you can substitute any berry to suit.

MAKES 24

Preparation time 5 minutes + chilling

125 ml (4 fl oz/½ cup) Coconut cream (page 17)
30 g (1 oz/½ cup) flaked coconut
1 tablespoon raw honey
½ teaspoon pure vanilla
80 ml (2½ fl oz/⅓ cup) coconut oil
125 g (4½ oz) blueberries

Line two 12-hole mini muffin tins with paper cases.

Blend the coconut cream, coconut, honey, vanilla and oil for **1 min/ speed 9**.

Divide the mixture evenly among the paper cases in the tin and top with the blueberries. Chill for 1 hour or until firm. Serve chilled.

DAIRY-FREE | GLUTEN-FREE | NUT-FREE | PALEO | VEGETARIAN

GINGERBREAD BISCUITS WITH COCONUT ICING

Ginger, coconut and raspberry all come together to make one pretty awesome little biscuit. Children love taking over with the icing (frosting) and topping with the raspberries – just prepare yourself for the fun and mayhem.

MAKES 18

Preparation time 10 minutes
Cooking time 20 minutes + cooling

225 g (8 oz/1 cup) whole wheat grains (see Note page 45)
60 g (2¼ oz) unsalted butter, chopped
125 ml (4 fl oz/½ cup) raw honey, plus 1 tablespoon extra
2 tablespoons pure maple syrup
2 teaspoons baking powder
1 tablespoon ground ginger
125 ml (4 fl oz/½ cup) Coconut cream (page 17)
80 ml (2½ fl oz/⅓ cup) coconut oil, melted, at room temperature
125 g (4½ oz) fresh raspberries, torn in half
flaked coconut, to serve

Preheat the oven to 180°C (350°F)/160°C (315°F) fan-forced. Line two large baking trays with baking paper.

Mill the wheat grains for **1 min/speed 10**. Transfer to a bowl.

Cook the butter, honey and maple syrup for **5 min/120°C/speed 2**.

Add the baking powder, ginger and reserved milled wheat. Mix for **1 min/speed 5**. Leave to cool in the mixer bowl for 20 minutes or until the mixture is firm.

Place firmly packed and level tablespoon measures of the sticky mixture onto the prepared trays, about 4 cm (1½ inches) apart to allow for spreading. Bake both trays on separate racks in the oven for 12–15 minutes, swapping the trays halfway during baking, or until light golden. Leave the biscuits to cool on the trays.

Mix the coconut cream, coconut oil and the extra honey for **20 sec/speed 4**. Spoon the coconut mixture evenly over the cooled biscuits. Top with the fresh raspberries and flaked coconut and serve.

NUT-FREE | VEGETARIAN

LEMON AND PASSIONFRUIT SLICE

The flavours in this slice (bar) always remind me of school fêtes when growing up. These are super-hardy, transportable morsels ideal for kids and perfect with a hot cup of tea. You can also swap the passionfruit pulp, when not in season, for either the Spiced plum spread (page 52) or Strawberry spread (page 53).

MAKES 12 PIECES

Preparation time 5 minutes
Cooking time 50 minutes + cooling

170 g (6 oz/¾ cup) whole wheat grains (see Note page 45)
55 g (2 oz/1 cup) flaked coconut
125 ml (4 fl oz/½ cup) raw honey
125 g (4½ oz) butter, at room temperature
125 ml (4 fl oz/½ cup) lemon juice
90 g (3 oz/⅓ cup) passionfruit pulp (see Note),
    plus whole passionfruit halves, to garnish
1 egg
finely grated lemon zest, to garnish

Preheat the oven to 160°C (315°F)/140°C (275°F) fan-forced. Line the base and sides of a 28 x 18 cm (11¼ x 7 inch) slab tin with baking paper.

Mill the wheat grains and coconut for **1 min/speed 10**. Scrape down the side of the bowl.

Add all the remaining ingredients and mix for **30 sec/speed 4**.

Transfer the mixture to the prepared tin, pressing down firmly to level the surface. Bake for 50 minutes or until cooked and golden. Leave to cool in the tin.

Transfer the slice to a board and cut into 12 pieces. Sprinkle with the lemon zest. Serve immediately with the passionfruit halves, or store in an airtight container at room temperature for up to 5 days.

NUT-FREE | VEGETARIAN

NOTE
You will need two heavy (or four light) passionfruit for the pulp.

CAROB AND RASPBERRY POPS

The avocado adds such a delicious creamy richness to these pops. If you have many moulds on hand, whip up some big batches of this so you always have a treat that children can easily help themselves to from the freezer. You will know it's packed full of goodness, but their tastebuds won't have a clue!

MAKES 6

Preparation time 5 minutes + freezing

120 g (4¼ oz) raspberries
1 ripe banana, peeled and broken into 3
1 small avocado, peeled and stoned
45 g (1½ oz/⅓ cup) carob powder
180 ml (6 fl oz/¾ cup) milk of choice (Vanilla pepita milk, page 16, or Coconut milk, page 17)

Place the raspberries into six 125 ml (4½ fl oz/½ cup) iceblock (popsicle/ice lolly) moulds. Set aside.

Blend the banana, avocado, carob powder and milk for **1 min/speed 9**.

Pour the banana mixture into the iceblock moulds over the raspberries, tapping each one down firmly on a work surface to release any air bubbles. Insert a wooden iceblock stick into the centre of each raspberry pop. Freeze for 2 hours or until firm. They will keep in the freezer for up to 6 months.

DAIRY-FREE | GLUTEN-FREE | NUT-FREE | VEGAN | VEGETARIAN

NOTE
If you don't happen to have any ripe bananas, but only firm ones, simply add 2 tablespoons pure maple syrup to the mixture to sweeten it.

KAFFIR LIME AND MANGO FROZEN YOGHURT

This is a beautiful frozen treat to enjoy after an Asian or Indian feast – or really on any day of the week!

SERVES 6

Preparation time 5 minutes + freezing

2 large mangoes, peeled, seeded and flesh roughly chopped
8 ripe bananas, peeled and broken into 3
2 kaffir lime leaves, centre stem removed, thinly shredded
500 ml (17 fl oz/2 cups) Cow's milk yoghurt (page 14)

Line two large baking trays with baking paper.

Place the mango and banana on the prepared trays in a single layer. Freeze for 1 hour or until firm.

Blend the frozen mango and banana, the lime leaves and yoghurt for **30 sec/speed 9**. Scrape down the side of the bowl. Blend again for **30 sec/speed 9**.

Serve immediately or freeze in an airtight container for up to 6 months.

GLUTEN-FREE | NUT-FREE | VEGETARIAN

PRETTY ICED BERRY PARFAITS

Too pretty, and also far too easy, for words. As long as you have all the fruit waiting in your freezer, this can literally be on the table in minutes. Guilt-free and oh so good for you.

SERVES 4

Preparation time 10 minutes

250 g (9 oz/2 cups) frozen blueberries, plus 60 g (2¼ oz/½ cup) extra
125 ml (4 fl oz/½ cup) cream of choice, plus 125 ml (4 fl oz/½ cup) extra
250 g (9 oz/2 cups) frozen raspberries, plus 60 g (2 oz/½ cup) extra
2 teaspoons rosewater
25 g (1 oz/¼ cup) toasted pecans, halved lengthways
dried edible rose petals, to serve

Blend the blueberries and cream for **20 sec/speed 9**. Scrape down the side of the bowl. Blend again for **20 sec/speed 9**.

Spoon the blueberry mixture into the base of four serving glasses. Top with half of the extra blueberries.

Blend the raspberries, rosewater and extra cream for **20 sec/speed 9**. Scrape down the side of the bowl. Blend again for **20 sec/speed 9**.

Spoon the raspberry mixture on top of the blueberries in the glasses. Top with the extra raspberries and then the remaining blueberries.

Top with the pecans and edible rose petals and serve immediately.

GLUTEN-FREE | VEGETARIAN

PIÑA COLADA NICE-CREAM

This recipe was gifted to me by a mum from daycare and was my first step into the world of using a mixer to save time in the kitchen. Honestly, this is the best afternoon treat for the family to share and, with just three ingredients and some slight effort, it really is a must to try.

SERVES 6

Preparation time 5 minutes + freezing

600 g (1 lb 5 oz) peeled, cored pineapple, cut into 3 cm (1¼ inch) pieces
6 ripe bananas, peeled, broken into 3
500 ml (17 fl oz/2 cups) Coconut cream (page 17)

Line two large baking trays with baking paper.

Place the pineapple and banana on the prepared trays in a single layer. Freeze for 1 hour or until firm.

Blend the frozen pineapple, frozen banana and coconut cream for **30 sec/speed 9**. Scrape down the side. Blend again for **30 sec/speed 9**. Serve immediately or freeze in an airtight container for up to 6 months.

DAIRY-FREE | GLUTEN-FREE | NUT-FREE | VEGAN | VEGETARIAN

HONEY AND LEMON SEMIFREDDO

I just love the idea that you can make a dessert like this up to 2 weeks ahead of serving it to guests and know that it's happily waiting in the freezer for you. It makes for ultimate stress-free party hosting. If you don't have a silicone loaf (bar) tin, simply double-line the base and sides of a standard loaf tin with baking paper.

SERVES 8

Preparation time 10 minutes
Cooking time 9 minutes + freezing

125 ml (4 fl oz/½ cup) lemon juice
125 ml (4 fl oz/½ cup) raw honey
6 egg yolks, at room temperature
fresh figs, to serve
fresh honeycomb, to serve
toasted pine nuts, to serve

Insert the whisk attachment inside the mixer bowl. Add all the ingredients and whisk for **9 min/70°C/speed 3**.

Pour the honey mixture into a 20 x 8 cm (8 x 3¼ inch) silicone loaf (bar) tin. Freeze for 4 hours or until firm.

Turn the semifreddo out onto a serving plate. Top with the figs, honeycomb and pine nuts and serve.

DAIRY-FREE | GLUTEN-FREE | PALEO | VEGETARIAN

NOTE

After taking it out of the freezer, let the semifreddo stand for a few minutes at room temperature, and use a serrated knife, to make slicing easier.

PUMPKIN SLAB PIE

Please, if you have never had the opportunity to try the delicious flavour of a pumpkin pie, give this pie a go. It's so creamy and decadent – I actually make this on Christmas Day and serve it alongside a traditional pudding. It makes a great winter dessert generally, with the warming spices and the creamy texture of the filling.

SERVES 8

Preparation time 15 minutes
Cooking time 55 minutes + cooling

1 quantity Macadamia pastry (page 22)
400 g (14 oz) peeled and seeded butternut pumpkin (winter squash), cut into 2 cm (¾ inch) pieces
375 ml (13 fl oz/1½ cups) Coconut cream (page 17)
2 eggs plus 3 egg yolks
125 ml (4 fl oz/½ cup) pure maple syrup
1 teaspoon mixed (pumpkin pie) spice
½ teaspoon ground ginger
freshly grated nutmeg, to serve
Nut cream (page 15), to serve

Line the base and sides of a 28 x 18 cm (11¼ x 7 inch) slab tin with baking paper.

Press the pastry evenly over the base and sides of the prepared tin, then chill until required.

Preheat the oven to 180°C (350°F)/160°C (315°F) fan-forced. Place a large baking tray in the oven to preheat.

Add 500 ml (17 fl oz/2 cups) water to the mixer bowl and attach the mixer bowl lid. Attach the steaming bowl, instead of the measuring cup, to the mixer bowl lid. Add the pumpkin to the steaming bowl and cover with the steaming bowl lid. Cook for **15 min/steam mode/speed 1**. Leave to stand until cool.

Mix all the remaining ingredients and the cooled pumpkin for **1 min/speed 4**.

Pour the pumpkin mixture over the pastry base in the prepared tin and level the surface. Bake in the tin set on the preheated baking tray in the oven for 40 minutes or until just set in the centre. Leave to cool in the tin.

Transfer to a board and cut into 8 pieces. Serve topped with the nutmeg and nut cream.

See photograph on pages 206–7.

DAIRY-FREE | GLUTEN-FREE | PALEO | VEGETARIAN

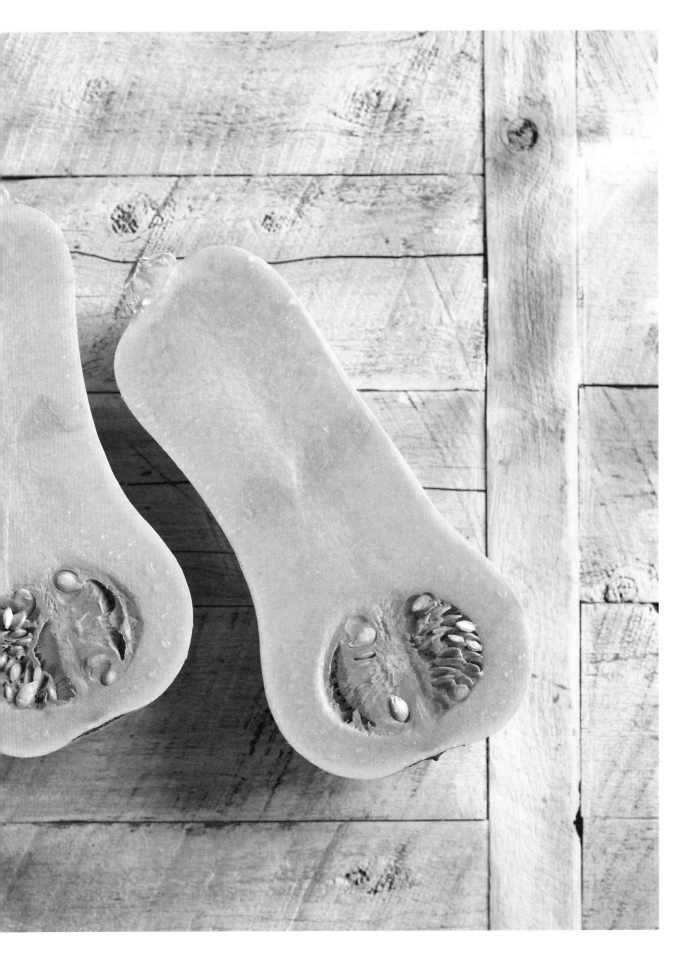

PUMPKIN SLAB PIE (PAGE 204)

FESTIVE SPICED STEAMED PUDDING

This contains the festive flavours of the Christmas season in one little pudding, but without the hours of boiling on the stovetop.

SERVES 6

Preparation time 10 minutes
Cooking time 1 hour 10 minutes
+ cooling

125 g (4½ oz) butter, at room
  temperature
240 g (8½ oz/1½ cups) whole
  natural almonds
1 small orange
1 whole clove
2 eggs
80 ml (2½ fl oz/⅓ cup)
  pure maple syrup,
  plus extra to serve
1 teaspoon mixed (pumpkin pie) spice
1 teaspoon ground ginger
¼ teaspoon ground cloves
thin (pouring/whipping) cream,
  to serve

Using some of the butter, grease a 750 ml (26 fl oz/3 cup) capacity ceramic pudding basin (mould) or heatproof glass bowl. Line the base with a small round of baking paper.

Mill the almonds for **20 sec/speed 9**.

Finely grate the zest of the orange and place it in the mixer bowl. Remove and discard the skin and white pith from the orange. Cut one 2 cm (¾ inch) thick slice from the orange. Insert the whole clove in the centre of the orange slice and place it in the base of the prepared basin.

Place the remaining orange flesh in the mixer bowl with the zest. Blend for **30 sec/speed 9**. Scrape down the side of the bowl.

Add the eggs, maple syrup, mixed spice, ginger, ground cloves and remaining butter. Mix for **30 sec/speed 5**. Spoon the orange mixture into the prepared basin, levelling the top. Place a round of baking paper on top.

Place 1.5 litres (52 fl oz/6 cups) water in the mixer bowl. Attach the steaming bowl, instead of the measuring cup, to the mixer bowl lid. Set the pudding basin inside the steaming bowl. Attach the steaming bowl lid. Steam for **70 min/steam mode/speed 2**. Leave to cool for 20 minutes before removing the pudding basin from the steaming bowl.

Carefully turn the pudding out onto a serving plate. Serve warm with the cream and extra maple syrup. Chill in an airtight container for up to 3 days.

GLUTEN-FREE |
VEGETARIAN

RHUBARB TART

This is a perfect gluten-free tart that's impressive when plated and equally good to eat. If transporting to a loved one or to take outdoors, simply leave it in the tin and transfer to a serving plate on arrival.

SERVES 6
Preparation time 15 minutes
Cooking time 35 minutes + cooling

coconut oil, for greasing
1 quantity Macadamia pastry
   (page 22)
115 g (4 oz/⅓ cup) walnuts
50 g (1¾ oz) butter, at room
   temperature
½ teaspoon pure vanilla
1 egg
2 tablespoons pure maple syrup,
   plus 1 tablespoon extra
finely grated zest and juice of
   1 small lemon
1 bunch rhubarb, washed,
   trimmed and cut into 8 cm
   (3¼ inch) lengths

Preheat the oven to 180°C (350°F)/160°C (315°F) fan-forced. Grease a 10 x 34 cm (4 x 13½ inch) tart (flan) tin with a removable base with coconut oil. Place a large baking tray in the oven to preheat.

Press the pastry evenly over the base and sides of the prepared tin. Trim away any excess pastry. Chill until required.

Mill the walnuts for **30 sec/speed 9**. Scrape down the side of the bowl.

Add the butter, vanilla, egg, maple syrup and lemon zest. Mix for **30 sec/speed 4**.

Transfer the walnut mixture to the pastry-lined tin, levelling the surface. Top with the rhubarb.

Combine the lemon juice and extra maple syrup, then brush half of this mixture over the top of the rhubarb.

Bake in the tin set on the preheated tray in the oven for 35 minutes or until set and golden. Brush with the remaining lemon juice mixture. Leave to cool in the tin for 5 minutes.

Carefully transfer the tart to a serving plate. Serve warm or at room temperature. Keep in an airtight container for up to 2 days.

GLUTEN-FREE | VEGETARIAN

HAZELNUT PEAR CRUMBLES

This is one for the kids and is a perfect-sized treat for dessert. It's great dolloped with a scoop of Kaffir lime and mango frozen yoghurt (page 199) or drizzled with cream. It just has to be eaten straight from the oven.

SERVES 4
Preparation time 15 minutes
Cooking time 20 minutes

4 firm green pears, halved lengthways and cored
1 tablespoon whole wheat grains (see Note page 45)
40 g (1½ oz/¼ cup) skinless hazelnuts
75 g (2¾ oz/¾ cup) rolled (porridge) oats
1 tablespoon carob powder
1 tablespoon pure maple syrup
50 g (1¾ oz) chilled butter, chopped

Preheat the oven to 220°C (425°F)/200°C (400°F) fan-forced. Line a large baking tray with baking paper.

Add 500 ml (17 fl oz/2 cups) water to the mixer bowl. Attach the steaming bowl, instead of the measuring cup, to the mixer bowl lid. Add the pear to the steaming bowl. Attach the steaming bowl lid. Steam for **10 min/steaming mode/speed 2**.

Transfer the pear to the prepared tray, cut side facing up. Clean and dry the mixer bowl.

Mill the wheat grains and hazelnuts for **1 min/speed 10**. Scrape down the side of the bowl.

Add all the remaining ingredients and mix gently for **1 min/dough mode**.

Spoon the hazelnut mixture on top of the pear on the prepared tray. Bake for 10 minutes or until golden and crisp. Serve.

VEGETARIAN

MOCHA CAKE WITH CHOCOLATE GANACHE

There's no reason to deprive yourself, or those you love, of a chocolate fix when you can make this seriously easy, yet beautifully presented cake. If pomegranates are not in season, simply adorn the cake with sliced strawberries or little jewel-like raspberries.

SERVES 8

Preparation time 10 minutes
Cooking time 50 minutes + cooling

340 g (11¾ oz/1½ cups) whole wheat grains (see Note page 45)
100 g (3½ oz) dark chocolate (70% cocoa solids), broken into pieces
125 g (4½ oz) butter, at room temperature
125 ml (4 fl oz/½ cup) pure maple syrup
2 eggs
2 teaspoons baking powder
80 ml (2½ fl oz/⅓ cup) espresso coffee, cooled
170 ml (5½ fl oz/⅔ cup) milk of choice
½ teaspoon pure vanilla
whipped cream, to serve
pomegranate seeds, to serve (see Note on page 30)

Chocolate ganache
100 g (3½ oz) dark chocolate (70% cocoa solids), broken into pieces
80 ml (2½ fl oz/⅓ cup) thin (whipping/pouring) cream

Preheat the oven to 160°C (315°F)/140°C (275°F) fan-forced. Line the base and side of a 20 cm (8 inch) round cake tin with baking paper.

Mill the wheat grains for **1 min/speed 10**. Scrape down the side of the bowl. Add the chocolate and mix for **10 sec/speed 8**. Scrape down the side of the bowl.

Add the remaining cake ingredients and mix for **20 sec/speed 4**.

Spoon the cake mixture into the prepared tin, levelling the surface. Bake for 50 minutes or until cooked and golden. Leave to cool in the tin. Transfer to a serving plate.

Meanwhile, to make the chocolate ganache, chop the chocolate for **10 sec/speed 8**. Scrape down the side of the bowl. Add the cream and cook for **2 min/50°C/speed 3**. Leave to cool in the mixer bowl for 20 minutes.

Spread the ganache over the cooled cake. Top the cake with the cream and pomegranate seeds and serve. Keep in an airtight container for up to 3 days.

NUT-FREE | VEGETARIAN

BUTTER CAKE WITH VANILLA FROSTING

Baking has never been easier than with this foolproof vanilla cake. The mixture will also make 12 cupcakes, which are perfect for little hands or as a party treat.

SERVES 8

Preparation time 10 minutes
Cooking time 50 minutes + cooling

340 g (11¾ oz/1½ cups) whole wheat grains (see Note page 45)
125 g (4½ oz) unsalted butter, at room temperature
125 ml (4 fl oz/½ cup) pure maple syrup
2 eggs
2 teaspoons baking powder
185 ml (6 fl oz/¾ cup) milk of choice
½ teaspoon pure vanilla
strawberries, hulled and halved, to serve

Vanilla frosting
150 g (5½ oz) unsalted butter, at room temperature
125 ml (4 fl oz/½ cup) raw honey
2 vanilla beans, split lengthways, seeds scraped

To make the cake, preheat the oven to 160°C (315°F)/140°C (275°F) fan-forced. Line the base and side of a 20 cm (8 inch) round cake tin with baking paper.

Mill the wheat grains for **1 min/speed 10**. Scrape down the side of the bowl.

Add the remaining ingredients and mix for **20 sec/speed 6**. Scrape down the side of the bowl. Mix again for **20 sec/speed 6**.

Spoon the cake mixture into the prepared tin, levelling the surface. Bake for 50 minutes or until cooked and golden. Leave to rest in the tin for 5 minutes, then transfer to a wire rack to cool completely.

To make the frosting, insert the whisk attachment inside the mixer bowl. Add the butter, honey and vanilla seeds. Whisk for **1 min/speed 4**.

Spread the frosting over the cooled cake. Top with the fresh strawberries and serve. Chill in an airtight container for up to 3 days.

NUT-FREE | VEGETARIAN

PINEAPPLE CARROT CAKE

Slightly hummingbird-ish, this super-moist, dense and lightly spiced cake is too good not to eat warm with lashings of Nut cream (page 15). If there happen to be leftovers, store them in an airtight container and chill for up to 3 days.

SERVES 12

Preparation time 10 minutes
Cooking time 1 hour 20 minutes + cooling

340 g (11¾ oz/1½ cups) whole wheat grains (see Note page 45)
100 g (3½ oz/½ cup) tapioca pearls
2 carrots, cut into 3
200 g (7 oz) pineapple, peeled, cored and cut into
    3 cm (1¼ inch) pieces
125 g (4½ oz) butter, at room temperature
3 eggs
80 ml (2½ fl oz/⅓ cup) pure maple syrup,
    plus 1 tablespoon extra
2 teaspoons baking powder
1 teaspoon mixed (pumpkin pie) spice
1 teaspoon ground cardamom
90 g (3¼ oz/¾ cup) walnuts

Preheat the oven to 180°C (350°F)/160°C (315°F) fan-forced. Line the base and side of a 20 cm (8 inch) round spring-form cake tin.

Mill the wheat grains and tapioca for **1 min/speed 10**. Transfer the mixture to a bowl and set aside.

Chop the carrot and pineapple for **5 sec/speed 5**. Scrape down the side of the bowl.

Add the butter, eggs, maple syrup, baking powder, mixed spice, cardamom and reserved milled wheat mixture. Mix for **20 sec/speed 5**.

Transfer the cake mixture to the prepared tin, levelling the surface. Top with the walnuts, then brush with the extra maple syrup. Bake for 1 hour 20 minutes or until cooked and golden, covering the cake loosely with a piece of foil halfway through baking time to prevent it from browning too quickly. Leave to cool in the tin for 20 minutes.

Carefully release the side of the tin and transfer the cake to a serving plate. Serve warm or at room temperature.

VEGETARIAN

RICOTTA APPLE PUFFS

Little golden puffs of deliciousness and almost doughnut-like in flavour and texture, these are the perfect pop-in-your-mouth sweet treat. It's very hard to stop at just one or two — especially when they're hot.

MAKES 24

Preparation time 10 minutes
Cooking time 10 minutes

coconut oil, softened, for greasing
170 g (6 oz/¾ cup) whole wheat grains (see Note page 45)
1 green apple, quartered and cored
230 g (8½ oz/1 cup) Fresh ricotta (page 12)
½ teaspoon pure vanilla
2 eggs
1 tablespoon raw honey
1 teaspoon baking powder
carob powder, for dusting

Preheat the oven to 200°C (400°F)/180°C (350°F) fan-forced. Liberally grease two 12-hole, 1 tablespoon measure mini muffin tins with coconut oil. Place in the oven to preheat.

Mill the wheat grains for **1 min/speed 10**. Scrape down the side of the bowl.

Add the apple and chop for **5 sec/speed 7**. Scrape down the side of the bowl.

Add all the remaining ingredients. Mix for **10 sec/speed 4**. Scrape down the side of the bowl. Mix again for **10 sec/speed 4**.

Very carefully remove the hot tins from the oven and fill them with the apple mixture. Bake for 10 minutes or until cooked, puffed and golden. Leave to stand for 3 minutes in the tin.

Transfer the puffs to a serving plate, dust with the carob powder and serve hot.

NUT-FREE | VEGETARIAN

HONEY SEEDED SLICE

A throwback to school day canteen treats, this chewy and very sweet seeded slice is still a great addition to lunchboxes – or your handbag.

MAKES 16 PIECES

Preparation time 5 minutes
Cooking time 10 minutes + chilling

250 ml (9 fl oz/1 cup) raw honey
80 g (2¾ oz) pepitas (pumpkin seeds)
50 g (1¾ oz) sunflower seeds
50 g (1¾ oz) linseeds (flaxseeds)
250 g (9 oz) sesame seeds

Line the base and sides of an 18 x 28 cm (7 x 11¼ inch) slab tin with baking paper.

Cook all the ingredients for **10 min/120°C/speed 2**.

Pour the hot mixture into the prepared tin. Using a heatproof spatula, press the seeded mixture firmly over the base of the tin. Leave to cool slightly, then chill for 1 hour or until almost set firm.

Transfer the slice to a board and cut into 16 pieces. Serve or chill in an airtight container for up to 1 week.

DAIRY-FREE | GLUTEN-FREE | NUT-FREE | PALEO | VEGETARIAN

BAKED DOUGHNUTS

Who doesn't love a hot doughnut? This recipe pays homage to a doughnut cookbook I wrote while heavily pregnant with my second child. Being baked, not fried, means that you get to devour these strawberry-filled gems with a fairly guilt-free conscience.

MAKES 12

Preparation time 30 minutes
Cooking time 20 minutes + cooling

55 g (2 oz/1 cup) flaked coconut
½ teaspoon ground cinnamon
560 g (1 lb 4 oz/2½ cups) whole
   wheat grains (see Note page 45)
40 g (1½ oz/¼ cup) tapioca pearls
3 teaspoons baking powder

80 g (2¾ oz) unsalted butter, at
   room temperature, plus 100 g
   (3½ oz) extra, melted
80 ml (2½ fl oz/⅓ cup) raw honey
1 egg plus 1 egg yolk
½ teaspoon pure vanilla
125 ml (4 fl oz/½ cup) milk of choice
Strawberry spread (page 53) and
   Nut cream (page 15), to serve

Preheat the oven to 180°C (350°F)/160°C (315°F) fan-forced. Line a large baking tray with baking paper.

Mill the coconut and cinnamon for **30 sec/speed 9**. Transfer to a small heatproof bowl.

Mill the wheat grains and tapioca pearls for **1 min/speed 10**. Scrape down the side of the bowl.

Add the baking powder, butter, honey, egg, egg yolk, vanilla and milk. Mix for **30 sec/speed 3**. Mix again for **30 sec/speed 3**.

Place ¼ cup measures of the mixture onto the prepared tray, shaping them into 6 cm (2½ inch) wide rounds. Bake for 10–20 minutes, or until cooked and golden. Immediately brush the tops with the melted butter and dip them into the coconut mixture in the bowl. Leave to cool for 10 minutes.

Split the doughnuts in half and fill with strawberry spread and nut cream. Serve the doughnuts warm or at room temperature.

VEGETARIAN

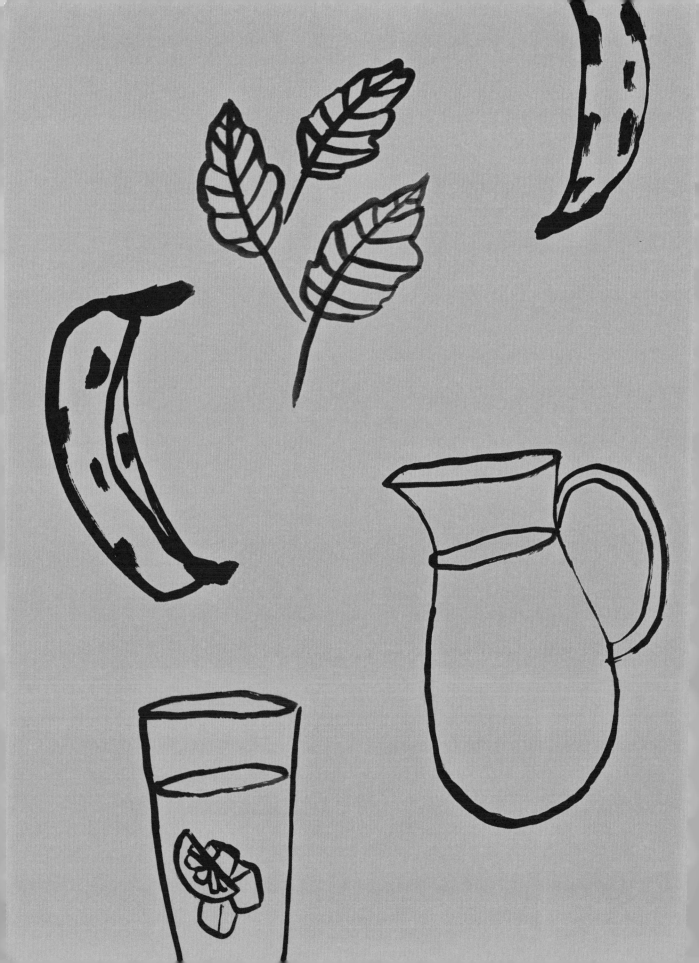

drinks,
smoothies
& shakes

BREAKFAST LEMON GINGER WATER

Nothing kick-starts your day, liver and digestion better than having a lovely warm mug of this. If I feel a tickly throat coming on I will also add some whole cloves. It's great all year round but best in the cooler months.

SERVES 2
Preparation time 5 minutes
Cooking time 3 minutes

1 small lemon, skin and white pith removed, chopped and seeded
4 cm (1½ inch) piece fresh ginger, peeled and halved
500 ml (17 fl oz/2 cups) water
2 cinnamon sticks
1 pinch cayenne pepper
2 teaspoons pure maple syrup

Blend the lemon and ginger for **10 sec/speed 7**. Scrape down the side of the bowl. Blend again for **10 sec/speed 5**.

Add all the remaining ingredients and cook for **3 min/120°C/speed 1**. Serve hot.

See photograph on pages 224–5.

DAIRY-FREE | GLUTEN-FREE | NUT-FREE | PALEO | VEGAN | VEGETARIAN

VARIATION

Add ¼–1 teaspoon Turmeric paste (page 33) for even more health benefits.

CASHEW HOT CHOC

So creamy and so delicious, this is a wonderful winter's day treat that the family will love. No one will ever guess that it has been made with cashew nuts rather than cream.

SERVES 4

Preparation time 5 minutes
Cooking time 5 minutes

155 g (5½ oz/1 cup) raw cashew nuts, soaked overnight in water, drained
750 ml (26 fl oz/3 cups) water
1 vanilla bean, halved lengthways, seeds scraped
35 g (1¼ oz/¼ cup) carob powder
2 teaspoons pure maple syrup

Cook all the ingredients for **5 min/90°C/speed 1**. Blend for **40 sec/speed 4**, slowly increasing to **speed 8**. Serve warm.

See photograph on pages 224–5.

DAIRY-FREE | GLUTEN-FREE | VEGAN | VEGETARIAN

SPICED
WINTER
COFFEE
(PAGE 226)

BREAKFAST
LEMON GINGER
WATER
(PAGE 222)

CASHEW HOT CHOC
(PAGE 223)

SPICED WINTER COFFEE

This is a lovely strong serve of coffee for two people – think of a strong long black. If you want to stretch to four people for a 'regular' coffee, then fill the rest of the serving cups with your milk of choice – preferably warmed. Other great spices to use include whole cloves, star anise and caraway seeds.

SERVES 2–4
Preparation time 5 minutes
Cooking time 3 minutes

45 g (1½ oz/½ cup) whole coffee beans
500 ml (17 fl oz/2 cups) water
6 cardamom pods, bruised
2 teaspoons fennel seeds
2 cinnamon sticks
milk of choice, to serve

Mill the coffee beans for **1 min/speed 9**. Scrape down the side of the bowl.

Add all the remaining ingredients and cook for **3 min/120°C/speed 1**. Leave to stand in the mixer bowl for 5 minutes.

Using a small fine-mesh sieve, strain the coffee mixture into two warmed serving cups. Discard the spices. Serve warm with a dash of milk.

See photograph on pages 224–5.

GLUTEN-FREE | NUT-FREE | VEGETARIAN

NOTE
While your coffee mixture is brewing, fill your serving cups with hot tap water to warm them up.

MOCHA SLUSHIE

An anytime-of-the-day, guilt-free 'treat'. This slushie is awesome on really hot summer mornings, as an afternoon pick-me-up or to drink while watching a movie marathon.

SERVES 4

Preparation time 5 minutes
Cooking time 3 minutes

45 g (1½ oz/½ cup) whole coffee beans
500 ml (17 fl oz/2 cups) Coconut cream (page 17)
30 g (1 oz/¼ cup) carob powder
2 tablespoons pure maple syrup
400 g (14 oz) small ice cubes

Mill the coffee beans for **1 min/speed 9**. Scrape down the side of the bowl.

Add the coconut cream and cook for **3 min/80°C/speed 1**.

Using a fine-mesh sieve, strain the milk mixture into a heatproof jug. Rinse the mixer bowl.

Return the strained milk mixture to the mixer bowl. Add all the remaining ingredients and blend for **1 min/speed 9**. Serve.

DAIRY-FREE | GLUTEN-FREE | NUT-FREE | VEGAN | VEGETARIAN

BREAKFAST SHAKE

Sometimes I will peel two long lengths of apple skin to top the children's shakes and call them 'apple snakes' – which they think is hilarious. But then I am quickly reminded by Mr 4-year-old that 'they are not real snakes, Mummy'.

SERVES 4

Preparation time 5 minutes

1 red apple, quartered and cored
50 g (1¾ oz/½ cup) rolled (porridge) oats
1 teaspoon ground cinnamon
1 tablespoon pure maple syrup
125 ml (4 fl oz/½ cup) Cow's milk yoghurt (page 14)
750 ml (26 fl oz/3 cups) Brown rice milk (page 16)

Chop the apple for **20 sec/speed 7**. Scrape down the side of the bowl. Add all the remaining ingredients. Blend for **1 min/speed 9** then serve.

See photograph on pages 230–1.

GLUTEN-FREE | NUT-FREE | VEGETARIAN

ARVO BUZZ SMOOTHIE

Beetroot is one of my favourite little additions to smoothie combos. It will give you an added buzz in the afternoon and it's also particularly good for easing stomach bloating.

SERVES 1

Preparation time 5 minutes

1 small beetroot (beet), skin scrubbed, cut into 8 wedges
1 small red apple, quartered and cored
2 celery stalks, cut into 4 cm (1½ inch) lengths
125 ml (4 fl oz/½ cup) water
5 ice cubes

Blend all the ingredients, except the ice, for **1 min/speed 9**.
Serve immediately over the ice.

See photograph on pages 230–1.

DAIRY-FREE | GLUTEN-FREE | NUT-FREE | PALEO | VEGAN | VEGETARIAN

BLUEBERRY
CHEESECAKE
SHAKE
(PAGE 223)

CARAMEL
NUT SHAKE
(PAGE 232)

ARVO BUZZ
SMOOTHIE
(PAGE 229)

BREAKFAST
SHAKE
(PAGE 228)

CARAMEL NUT SHAKE

Yes, yes and yes! This is a real winner and a shake to satisfy even the sweetest of sweet tooths. Add a pinch of sea salt for a delicious salted caramel version. Be sure to serve the shake with spoons for scooping.

SERVES 4

Preparation time 5 minutes

80 ml (2½ fl oz/⅓ cup) Nut cream (page 15)
750 ml (26 fl oz/3 cups) Coconut milk (page 17)
½ teaspoon pure vanilla
1 tablespoon pure maple syrup
4 medjool dates, halved and pitted
135 g (4¾ oz/1 cup) small ice cubes

Blend all the ingredients with 250 ml (8½ fl oz/1 cup) water for **1 min/ speed 9**. Serve immediately.

See photograph on pages 230–1.

DAIRY-FREE | GLUTEN-FREE | PALEO | VEGAN | VEGETARIAN

BLUEBERRY CHEESECAKE SHAKE

It might sound strange to add ricotta to this shake, but please trust me – the delicate flavour of the ricotta is cheesecake-like when paired with the blueberries in this shake and oh so creamy. The chia seeds will keep you feeling full all the way through that mid-morning munchies stage, too. It's a win, win.

SERVES 4

Preparation time 5 minutes

1 tablespoon chia seeds
80 g (2¾ oz/½ cup) whole natural almonds
750 ml (26 fl oz/3 cups) milk of choice
   (try Vanilla pepita milk, page 16)
230 g (8½ oz/1 cup) Fresh ricotta (page 12)
2 tablespoons raw honey
125 g (4½ oz/1 cup) frozen blueberries

Blend all the ingredients for **1 min/speed 9**. Serve.

See photograph on pages 230–1.

GLUTEN-FREE | VEGETARIAN

NOTE

I prefer to freeze my own blueberries. I simply place the berries in flat freezer-safe, resealable bags for easy stacking in the freezer.

INDEX

ABOUT THE AUTHOR

Tracey Pattison is a cookbook author, food editor, food stylist and recipe writer, and has formerly worked in the Murdoch Books Test Kitchen. She is a qualified health coach with a passion for whole foods and encouraging families to make great, affordable meals that people of all ages will enjoy.

'Through my "real food" recipes and holistic approach to cooking and eating you can see how easy it is to incorporate seasonal whole foods into your daily life that will nourish you Mind, Body and Soul. Helping you to feel empowered, energised and connected.'

PUBLISHED IN 2017 BY MURDOCH BOOKS,
AN IMPRINT OF ALLEN & UNWIN

Murdoch Books Australia
83 Alexander Street
Crows Nest NSW 2065
Phone: +61 (0) 2 8425 0100
Fax: +61 (0) 2 9906 2218
murdochbooks.com.au
info@murdochbooks.com.au

Murdoch Books UK
Ormond House
26–27 Boswell Street
London WC1N 3JZ
Phone: +44 (0) 20 8785 5995
murdochbooks.co.uk
info@murdochbooks.co.uk

For Corporate Orders & Custom Publishing,
contact our Business Development Team
at salesenquiries@murdochbooks.com.au.

Publisher: Jane Morrow
Editorial Manager: Emma Hutchinson
Design Manager: Madeleine Kane
Project Editor: Ariana Klepac
Designer: Arielle Gamble
Photographers: Steve Brown and Alan Benson
Stylist: Tracey Pattison
Additional styling: Rhianne Contreras
Production Manager: Rachel Walsh

Text © Tracey Pattison 2017
The moral rights of the author have
been asserted.
Design © Murdoch Books 2017
Photography © Steve Brown 2017, pages 4–5, 13,
24, 31, 41, 44, 63, 71, 75, 79, 81, 84, 98, 130, 135,
139, 151, 155, 157, 161, 165, 173, 179, 183, 187, 188,
193, 201, 210, 217
Photography © Alan Benson 2017, pages 2, 6, 9,
18-19, 49, 50–1, 54, 59, 67, 89, 90–1, 95, 103, 109,
110–11, 115, 119, 123, 124–5, 146, 167, 168–9, 197,
205, 206–7, 213, 224–5, 230–1

A cataloguing-in-publication entry is available
from the catalogue of the National Library of
Australia at nla.gov.au.

ISBN 978 1 74336 865 7 Australia
ISBN 978 1 74336 869 5 UK

A catalogue record for this book is available
from the British Library.

Colour reproduction by Splitting Image
Colour Studio Pty Ltd, Clayton, Victoria
Printed by 1010 Printing International Limited,
China

DISCLAIMER: The purchaser of this book
understands that the operating information
contained within is not intended to replace the
thermo appliance instructions supplied by the
manufacturer. The author and publisher claim
no responsibility to any person or entity for
any liability, loss, damage or injury caused or
alleged to be caused directly or indirectly as a
result of the use, application or interpretation
of the material in this book. It is understood that
you will carefully follow the safety instructions
supplied by the manufacturer before operating
your thermo appliance.

IMPORTANT: Those who might be at risk from
the effects of salmonella poisoning (the elderly,
pregnant women, young children and those
suffering from immune deficiency diseases)
should consult their doctor with any concerns
about eating raw eggs.

Raw honey should not be consumed by infants
less than one year of age. Honey can contain
spores of a bacterium called Clostridium
botulinum, which can germinate in a baby's
immature digestive system and cause infant
botulism, a rare but potentially fatal illness.
In adults and children over 12 months, the
microorganisms normally found in the intestine
keep this bacteria from growing.

MEASURES GUIDE: We have used 20 ml
(4 teaspoon) tablespoon measures. If you are
using a 15 ml (3 teaspoon) tablespoon add
an extra teaspoon of the ingredient for each
tablespoon specified.